This Note's for You

This Note's for You

Popular Music + Advertising = Marketing Excellence

David Allan

BUSINESS EXPERT PRESS

First published in 2015 by
Business Expert Press, LLC
222 East 46th Street, New York, NY 10017
www.businessexpertpress.com

ISBN-13: 978-1-63157-001-8 (paperback)
ISBN-13: 978-1-63157-002-5 (e-book)

Business Expert Press Digital and Social Media Marketing and Advertising Collection

Collection ISSN: 2333-8822 (print)
Collection ISSN: 2333-8830 (electronic)

Cover and interior design by Exeter Premedia Services Private Ltd., Chennai, India

First edition: 2015

10 9 8 7 6 5 4 3 2 1

Printed in the United States of America.

Abstract

From Coca-Cola to Chrysler this book takes you behind the curtain of some of the best popular music in advertising campaigns of all time. Did you know that fog played a critical role in the "I'd Like to Teach the World to Sing" campaign, and that the choir had no idea that Eminem was going to show up while they were taping the "Lose Yourself" campaign, or that The Doors were supposed to be in the Cadillac commercials, not Led Zeppelin, until one of The Doors discovered that Cadillac made the Escalade and suddenly declined because he felt it was environmentally unfriendly. This book talks of the people who created the campaigns with the songs we remember the most. Everything from Bob Seger's "Like A Rock" (Chevy Trucks) to LMFAO's Party Rock and the dancing hamsters (Kia). The result is a book that educates and entertains on what made these campaigns excellent and how to make excellent campaigns. This collection of award-winning music in advertising campaigns is not available together anywhere else. It shows where this art in advertising form has been, where it is now, and provides the foundation for where it will go.

Keywords

advertising, commercials, marketing, popular music

Ain't singin' for Pepsi,
Ain't singin' for Coke,
I don't sing for nobody,
Makes me look like a joke,
This note's for you.

—Neil Young, **This Note's for You**.
Words and Music by Neil Young
© 1987 Silver Fiddle Music
All Rights Reserved Used by Permission
Reprinted by Permission Hal Leonard Corporation

Contents

Opening Act: The Brands

If you have had any marketing education or training you have undoubtedly heard of the four Ps (say it with me now: "Product, Price, Place, and Promotion"). Well, I am here to suggest that the brands in this book follow the four Ms ("Music Makes Marketing Magic"). In fact, there may be more than four Ms. You will see that the last M also means *Memorable, Mystical, Measureable, Manageable,* and, of course, *Money.*

In this book you will meet:

Paul Chibe, former CMO of US Marketing of Anheuser-Busch InBev (the company that believes that the "the enjoyment of great music is inspired by a love of great beer"[1]), the father of music of Budweiser's Made in America and both Budweiser Super Bowl commercials with popular music ("Landslide" and "Let Her Go"). In the case of "Let Her Go," this was the third most *memorable* ad in this year's Super Bowl according to marketingcharts.com.[2]

Michael Sprague (he was on NBC's "The Voice"), current EVP of Kia (the company with the "pack of music-loving hamsters"[3]), who called the commercials "a bit *magical*."[4] He uses music to attract Millennials. "We've become a really cool product that people have started to notice."[5] "It is clear that music and pop culture, indeed, has played a key role in Kia's resurgence."[6] Kia sales were up 9.8 percent in 2009.[7]

Olivier Francois, current CEO of Chrysler and CMO, who convinced Eminem to license "Lose Yourself" because both brand and artist were "imported from Detroit." How many CEOs you know can direct "the crescendo leading into Eminem's line: 'This is the Motor City. This is what we do'" as Francios did. To which the commercial's producer, Luis Resto, remarked: "How many car marketing guys can sit down and tell you why he wants a 'melancholy piano'… that was a first for me."[8]

And the guy with the toughest job in America, Ed Razek, CMO for Victoria's Secret, who did the unthinkable. He asked Bob Dylan to be in a commercial with a beautiful woman in Venice, Italy, with one of his own classic songs and Dylan said yes. He knew what he wanted. "We put a number of tracks against the commercial, and nothing worked except Dylan," Razek said, "In a very few words *manages* to sum up every relationship."[9]

You will see that these ads make *money*—for brand (sales) and the band (publishing and licensing). And you will learn how Worldwide Synchronization Licensing Revenues are as follows: 2006 ($2.1 billion), 2007 ($2.2 billion), 2008 ($2.3 million), 2009 ($2.4 billion), 2010 ($2.4 billion), 2011 ($2.5 billion), 2012 ($2.6 billion), 2013 ($2.5 billion) according to eMarketer).[10]

It is clear that these brands like it. For some, like American Express, it is "part of their marketing DNA."[11] For others, popular music makes "our brain sing."[12]

Finally, this book will lead by example. Every chapter will begin with the story of the campaign and end with, what else, *notes* summarizing the major points that not only made these ads excellent (according to me), but could help the musician or marketer make beautiful music in advertising too!

Synchronization and Transcription Licenses

A *synchronization license* (also called a *synch* [pronounced "sink"] license) is a license to use music in *timed synchronization* with visual images. A classic example is a song in a motion picture, where the song is synchronized with the action on the screen. It also includes television commercials, home video devices, and so on. Interestingly, it doesn't include radio commercials (since they're not synchronized with visuals). Radio commercial licenses are called *transcription licenses.*

The *fees* for synchronization licenses are really all over the board, and they vary with the usage and the importance of the song. An example of the lowest end would be 10-second background use of an unknown song in a television show (perhaps played on a jukebox while the actors are talking and ignoring it). A high-end example would be an on-camera, full-length performance of a well-known song in a major studio's high-budget film. And when we get into the realm of commercials, the fees go even higher.

For *commercials*, a song can get anywhere from $50,000 to $200,000 for a one-year national usage in the United States, on television and radio. Well-known songs in major campaigns can go higher, sometimes over a million for a classic, iconic song, but the current trend is downward. These figures get scaled down for regional or local usage, and for periods of less than a year.

CHAPTER 1

"Teach the World to Sing"
... Coca Cola (1971)

"I'd Like to Buy the World a Coke" had its origins on January 18, 1971, in a London fog. Bill Backer, creative director on the Coca-Cola account for the McCann-Erickson advertising agency, was flying to London to meet up with Billy Davis, the music director on the Coca-Cola account, to write radio commercials with two successful British songwriters, Roger Cook and Roger Greenaway, to be recorded by the New Seekers, a popular British singing group. The heavy fog in London forced the plane to land in Shannon, Ireland. Passengers had to remain near the airport in case the fog lifted. Some of them were furious about their accommodations. By the next day, Backer saw some of the most irate passengers in the airport cafe. Brought together by a common experience, many were now laughing and sharing stories over snacks and bottles of Coca-Cola. Bill Backer wrote of the scene: "In that moment [I] saw a bottle of Coke in a whole new light... [I] began to see a bottle of Coca-Cola as more than a drink that refreshed a hundred million people a day in almost every corner of the globe. So [I] began to see the familiar words, "Let's have a Coke," as more than an invitation to pause for refreshment. They were actually a subtle way of saying, "Let's keep each other company for a little while." And [I] knew they were being said all over the world as [I] sat there in Ireland. So that was the basic idea: to see Coke not as it was originally designed to be—a liquid refresher—but as a tiny bit of commonality between all peoples, a universally liked formula that would help to keep them company for a few minutes." When he finally arrived in London, Backer told Billy Davis and Roger Cook what he had seen in the airport café. After he expressed his thoughts about buying everybody in the world a Coke, Backer noticed that Davis's initial reaction was not at all what he'd expected and asked him, "Billy, do you have a problem with this idea?" Davis slowly revealed his problem. "Well, if I could do something for everybody in the world, it would not be to buy them a Coke." Backer responded, "What would you do?" "I'd buy everyone a home first and share with them in peace and love," Davis said. Backer said, "Okay, that sounds good. Let's write that and I'll show you how Coke fits right into the concept." A chord structure and the beginnings of the melody for the song had been written and recorded on a cassette tape, played on a ukulele, the previous year by Roger Greenway and Roger Cook. While waiting for Bill Backer to arrive from Ireland, Billy Davis and Roger Greenway had begun to develop ideas for radio jingles. Greenway pulled out the tape he and Cook had worked on and played a variety of melodies for Davis. Davis loved one of the melodies and he and Roger Greenway expanded on the melody, added a bridge and wrote a jingle called "Mom, True Love, and Apple Pie." When Bill Backer finally arrived in London, Billy Davis and Roger Cook played the material they had been working on for him. Backer loved the melody for "Mom, True Love, and Apple Pie," and suggested using it for what later became "I'd Like to Buy the World a Coke." The four song writers were all accomplished in their craft. Bill Backer had written the Coca-Cola jingle "Things Go Better with Coke" as well as the jingle for "The Real Thing" Coke campaign. Billy Davis, Roger Cook and Roger Greenaway were songwriters on many hits of the 1960s. Davis wrote Jackie Wilson's "Reet Petite" and "Lonely Teardrops," and Roger Cook and Roger Greenaway wrote pop standards including "Long Cool Woman (In A Black Dress)" and "You've Got Your Troubles and I've Got Mine." Working through the night, they crafted the song and, within a few days, Davis produced "I'd Like to Buy the World a Coke" along with two other commercials he wrote with Backer, Cook and Greenaway for The New Seekers. On February 12, 1971, "I'd Like to Buy the World a Coke" was shipped to radio stations around America. While some of the feedback from the Coca-Cola bottlers was not encouraging, many of Billy Davis's DJ friends from his record business career began to call him. They were saying things like, "I'm getting requests to play your commercial like it was a hit record" and "You should record it as a record." Bill Backer put his creative team to work to come up with a visual concept for "I'd Like to Buy the World a Coke." Out of the many creative ideas, the one that stood out was the one called "The First United Chorus of the World" created by art director Harvey Gabor. This concept featured young people all around the world singing together on a hillside. Backer presented the storyboards to The Coca-Cola Company and Coke advertising manager Ike Herbert approved more than $100,000 to film it. Phil Messina, the agency's producer, planned the filming of Gabor's visual concept on the cliffs of Dover. Hundreds of British schoolchildren and 65 principals were cast to lip-sync the song. Three days of continuous rain scrubbed the shoot. The crew moved to Rome. New young people were cast and taught by Davis to lip-sync the song. The opening shot of the commercial had to have that "right" face, which was filled by a young lady on vacation in Rome from Mauritius. The production was delayed by more rain. Finally, late in the day, the crew completed the climactic helicopter shot. The next day revealed that the young people looked as though they had really been in a rainstorm. The film was unusable, the budget was spent and the young people were released to go on their way. Because of Bill Backer's confidence in the hillside concept, Sid McAlister, the account supervisor on the Coke account, went to bat on another budget to re-shoot the spot, and McCann-Erickson tried again. The new budget eventually topped $250,000, a staggering amount in that era. Five hundred young people were hired for the chorus from embassies and schools in Rome. This was a substantial reduction from the original rained-out chorus. A British governess Davis and Gabor found pushing a baby carriage in the Piazza Navona was hired for the lead female role. The Italian film company Roma Film filmed the commercial and this time the weather cooperated. Close-ups of the young "leads" were actually filmed at a racetrack in Rome, separate from the larger chorus shots. Some of the distinctive camera angles were forced on the crew as they tried to avoid power and telephone lines. "I'd Like to Buy the World a Coke" was released in the U.S. in July 1971 and immediately struck a responsive chord. The Coca-Cola Company and its bottlers received more than 100,000 letters about the commercial. Many listeners called radio stations begging to hear it. Billy Davis wanted to produce a record version of the commercial with the New Seekers, but the group's manager claimed they didn't have time in their schedule to do so. Davis allowed a group of studio singers to record the new song lyric to "I'd Like to Buy the World a Coke." They called themselves "The Hillside Singers" in order to identify with the TV image. Within two weeks of the release of the Hillside Singers recording, it was on the national charts. Two weeks after that, Davis was able to convince the New Seekers to find the time and record their version of "I'd Like to Teach the World to Sing (in Perfect Harmony)," the new title for the song version of "I'd Like to Buy the World a Coke." He took them to the studio on a Sunday and produced the record which became the Top 10 hit, followed by the Hillside Singers' version as No. 13 on the pop charts. The song was recorded in a wide range of languages and sold more sheet music than any song in the previous 10 years. The Coca-Cola Company donated the first $80,000 in royalties earned from the song by writers and publishers to UNICEF under an agreement with the writers. "I'd Like to Buy the World a Coke" has had a lasting connection with the public. The commercial has consistently been voted one of the best of all time and the sheet music continues to sell today. The song version is being sung in school glee clubs and church choirs and played by high school bands all over the world. Thirty years after Bill Backer was stranded by fog, Coca-Cola is still more than a beverage. It is a common connection between the people of the world.[1]

Bill Backer clearly was a man on a mission with a vision and a wide-angle lens. He was charged with creating an advertising campaign. He knew that Robert W. Woodruff, the then head of Coca-Cola, believed that "the purpose of Coca-Cola advertising is to be liked."[2] He could have just made a likeable commercial like so many before and after it. Something smart and clever that some would have gotten and some would not. But that's not the way Backer grew up. His idols were "the song writers who wrote for the masses not the classes."[3] And besides he never thought "clever was as good as thoughtful."[4] He decided to take the Coca-Cola signature "five note melody"[5] and make instead, what he called, a "song-form commercial."[6] The rest is history. Was it luck? Backer believes that "you [should] give Lady Luck a chance to be your friend."[7] They evidently turned out to be best friends.

To this day, Teach the World to Sing is still the background music for the Coca Cola brand. Joe Belliotti, Director of Entertainment Marketing at Coca-Cola said:

> I think there is very rarely a time that we talk about Coke and music that we don't look back at "Teach the World to Sing," and the impact it made. The cultural impact, but more the pop cultural impact, the fact that it was very successful song and it created this moment and I think it was ... [and] I think it is always the bar which we strive to achieve because it did work so well. It was a great song, it was great idea, it has the right cultural context underneath it to bring the people together through music and it is very rare that we don't look at that and we always share that as one of the examples with new talent

that work with of how Coke really brings to life the brand through music.[8]

When asked for the importance of music to the Coca-Cola brand, Belliotti said music is who they are and have always been.

It always part of the Coke Cola DNA and I think what we try to do is express the brands through music and so how do you express the optimism, the happiness, the togetherness of Coke music? And that to me hasn't changed. That was indicative of the hilltop spot which was very much about bringing people together, with optimism and happiness and it is very much what we continue to do. So we are consistent in the fact that we want to find the right expression of the brands through music and so the programs we treat even today still have that idea of happiness and optimism and togetherness worded in everything that we are doing.[9]

When asked how Coca-Cola has been so successful integrating popular music in their branding, Belliotti said it was simple. "It's finding a talent that embodies the optimism, happiness of Coca-Cola and finding talent that loves Coke."[10] Bill Backer was that talent in 1971.

I always thought Coke Cola had kind of have a little lift that helped daily life go a little better and I still believe that of it. So it was easy to add a personality to a product promise or party promise, it was basically true. You can't push these things too hard over a long period and this is basically based on truth. A song can let you do that because it allows for repetition and it allows for both sort of practical facts stating a little bit and emotion and I think basically branding has to do with personality and emotion as much as it has to do with facts, you got to have both.[11]

When asked to comment on today's advertising he felt that too many had what he called "misapplied emotions."[12] Backer believes that commercials today are so busy focusing on attitude rather than product promises. It's such a different world. Songs were wonderful when you wanted to do something that was a long term image or brand. There was never, in my opinion a better medium for branding a product than music because branding takes time and it takes the ability to have certain amount of frequency. You don't get tired of a good song. People don't even understand branding. Brand is what you are and you can put in a personality, you can tighten it up but still has to have to be based on some basic truth.[13]

When asked what were the keys to creating excellent popular in music campaigns, Backer believes the song created or chosen is the key.

There are certain songs that are iconic but I don't think that necessarily would want to push a product with. I don't think I would ever take, "I get tired and fear to die, tired of living and fear of dying," I don't think I would ever say, I stopped and have a Coke after that. There are certain songs I wouldn't use them to amplify products advantages and others it would fit perfectly.[14]

Finally, when asked if he would rather be remembered as an ad man or songwriter he said both. "I had my cake and ate it too I guess because people still many generations my junior still remember the commercial and the song."[15]

1. "Music is the perfect medium for branding a product because branding takes time and it takes the ability to have certain amount of frequency. You don't get tired of a good song." Bill Backer
2. "Focus on the product not just the attitude. Be thoughtful, not just clever." Bill Backer
3. "The cultural impact, but more the pop cultural impact, the fact that it was very successful song and it created this moment." Joe Belliotti

"Teach the World to Sing" Commercial Lyrics

On a hilltop in Italy
We assembled young people
From all over the world
To bring you this message
From Coca-Cola bottlers
All over the world
It's the real thing—Coke.
And They Sang:
I'd like to buy the world a home
And furnish it with love
Grow apple trees and honey bees
And snow white turtle doves
(Chorus)
I'd like to teach the world to sing
In perfect harmony
I'd like to buy the world a Coke
And keep it company
That's the real thing
(Repeat Chorus)
(Chorus 2)
What the world wants today
Is the real thing
(Repeat Chorus 2)

CHAPTER 2

New Generation ... Michael Jackson and Pepsi (1983)

In November 1983, one year after Thriller was released, [Michael] Jackson (with his brothers) and PepsiCo struck a $5 million partnership that would shatter the record for a celebrity endorsement deal, link the two entities for a decade and set the bar for every integrated marketing campaign that would follow.[1]

The Jacksons wanted to align the band (and their famous brother Michael) with a brand. They hired Jay Colemen from Entertainment Marketing and Communications International who went to Coca-Cola first.

"They gave it serious consideration yet couldn't make that leap of faith," Coleman says. "They saw anything they would do with Michael as a more targeted, ethnic campaign." Coca-Cola offered a $1 million deal that was rejected and the Jacksons moved on to PepsiCo, where then-CEO Roger Enrico was looking for a big idea to launch his youth-targeted "New generation" campaign for the brand.[2]

When asked about how it all came about former Pepsi CEO Roger Enrico remembered:

I asked our head of advertising, Alan Pottasch, and the creative director of BBDO, Phil Dusenberry if they would do something for me. They had done the original "Pepsi Generation." I said, "You made history once, let's do it again." He said, "What do you want?" and I said, "I don't know but I just want something totally different." They came up with this "New Generation" idea. Phil's idea was to get the best directors and make mini-movies. His thing was always "put a smile on their face and a tug at their heart." That was the idea of each commercial. We went on and did it and it had never been done. A guy named Jay Coleman had a company called Rockbill and he kind of was in the business of putting corporations and rock stars together and he called me one day and said "Look, we can get you Michael Jackson," and I said, "Oh yes, right." He convinced me that it was possible and I thought I had seen the roughs of the commercials that Bill had done and they were great but I thought gee nobody is going to notice these things we need something big to bring attention to them. So I thought that the Jackson idea was perfect. And then, of course, Don King was the guy who was actually putting it together.[3]

When asked if Michael rewrote the song as has been reported Enrico said:

Someone else re-wrote the song. We had another song and a Jackson-look-alike when they took out the storyboards to show them … Phil said the guys loved it, and they were laughing like hell they thought they loved it and at the end Michael said, very politely, "Look it is very nice but I don't like the music and I don't like the song and I don't like the commercial." Why don't you use

Billy Jean. So Phil got somebody to re-write it and laid it down and it came out good.[4]

When asked if Michael was on board at the taping, as had been widely reported, Enrico said:

> I wasn't at the shoot actually but I can tell you that I know from what the guys told me they had a lot of trouble with Michael. He didn't drink Pepsi, we were lucky if we could get him to hold the bottle. He wasn't sure he wanted to do this and he was nervous about it, that he was kind of selling out. Things like he didn't want to take his sunglasses off, silly things like that. But they finally got him to do it. And after the commercials were done Michael and I had many many phones calls about editing. He was very nervous about, nervous about being over-exposed. So anyhow we worked it out over a long period of time. I almost scrapped the whole thing, out of frustration, but finally we got it done and he was happy with it then, once he saw the increase in sales of Thriller by a lot, once it went on the air. There was so much publicity about it that before we bought one commercial every news program in the country ran it free and MTV ran a world premiere commercial for nothing.[5]

Then came the fire.

> There was a little dispute over that. His lawyer, John Branca said that Michael is going to sue you guys and I said, "For what?" and

he said, "Pain and suffering and loss of income." I said "There can't be loss of income because I know the record sales went up it after it went on-the-air." So he just laughed at that. After several discussions about it he said, "Look you have to understand Michael is going to donate whatever you give to the burn center, He will match whatever you give." So we did it and I forget how much we gave maybe a million dollars. I don't remember exactly and Michael matched it. And we went out to the burn center and presented the check. So he was happy then. The next time around when they did BAD, they came to us. Michael and his manager came to us. They know it was good for the business, their business.[6]

When asked if Michael Jackson was happy with the campaign, Enrico said:

I spoke to him about a year before he died and he was working on his come back and, of course, I was out of Pepsi and so we weren't talking about him doing commercials again although I would have done then, I think, had I been there. Well, after picking the song, the effect on the record sales and Michael's tour went even more to the stratosphere, that whole thing about selling out went away. It really was a beautiful commercial.[7]

When asked if Michael Jackson was surprised by anything, Enrico confessed:

We did two versions, we did one with what you call the Street where there was a young boy Alfonso Ribeiro who was mimicking Michael and dancing in the street doing the moon walk and he bumped into Michael and he was shocked. Then there was another one where the fire happened, we called the cops in, where we practiced right out of a drive in LA with a bunch of kids and Michael didn't know that and thought he was just going to do a number and a shoot and when he came out and he saw the tents and he went crazy and, of course, he was so nervous with the fire too. He didn't see the kids. Our guys always did that something that, something to surprise the talent so that they would react naturally in a good way.[8]

When asked about the difference between Pepsi and Coca-Cola in general, Enrico said:

Coke kinda owned mainstream America and mother and apple pie and we had to be different to stand out. Our strategy was to be on the leading edge of cultural change and to target young adults, 17 to 22, that was the target. Figuring that older people would be fascinated by what younger people would do and kids would always look up to those 17 years. So you get everybody by doing that. That is the reason that we went to the music. It wasn't a strategy to be music marketing, although Coleman tried to get us to do that. We ended up doing that just by happen stance. First of all, get Michael to get attention to the campaign and then get Lionel Richie because Coke was about to sign him. And then one thing led to another, and we were going from one star to another star.[9]

When asked if it was true that Michael went to Coke first, Enrico said, "That's what I understand, they said there was an interesting 'ethnic opportunity' but Michael was hardly ethnic, I mean yes he was but he appealed to everyone, internationally he was even more than the US." Enrico confirmed that Pepsi paid Michael $5 million dollars. When asked how Coke used popular music in advertsing compared to Pepsi, Enrico said, "It was a little funky, they used Wham one time, it was kind of a mediocre rip off of our commercials, but didn't really get there, didn't have Phil Dusenberry that's why." And how did Pepsi pick the artists? Enrico said,

the first this is what you said, they had to be the hottest artists at the time. That was important and then they had a good clean appeal to not too edgy. Michael wasn't edgy. Brittany Spears wasn't edgy, she got the edgy later. Lionel was never edgy. [10]

Finally, when asked what made this popular music in advertising campaign excellent, Enrico gave credit to the creative team:

The first thing I think is that Dusenberry is a genius, a creative genius and did a fabulous job, he and his team. So those were really great mini-movies. You know we did kind of take a lot of inspiration from movies that were out. During one commercial it looked like Close Encounters, another commercial looked like ET, so much so that after we were on-the-air, I got a call from Steven Spielberg's lawyer saying he would like to see all of the commercials because we think you are ripping him off. Then we got a call from Steven saying, "These commercials are wonderful, be my guest." He was flattered. I think it did really break through the consciousness of the public at that time. Even now you go onto and see the commercials have millions of hits on YouTube, they're from 1984, it is almost thirty years now.[11]

When asked what makes popular music in advertising campaigns excellent, Enrico said:

The first thing is to think big but have a good strategy and if you got a strategy and a target audience, and you know how it reaches them. Think big and don't worry the costs, if you have good talent to do the creative.[12]

1. "Always put a smile on their face and a tug at their heart." Roger Enrico
2. "Think big and have a good strategy." Roger Enrico
3. "Don't worry about the costs." Roger Enrico

Note

Pepsi's marketing gurus have been appealing to consumers through music seemingly for eons. Much of that perception is due to the success the soda maker has had in tying its name to the King of

Pop, Michael Jackson. Even after the guy's been laid to rest for more than three years, and earning more than ever, Pepsi is still celebrating its legendary association with the performer. Back in May, Pepsi announced its deal with the Michael Jackson estate and Sony Music to an exclusive global marketing partnership that included featuring the Gloved One on a billion limited edition Pepsi cans released around the world, starting in China.[13]

CHAPTER 3

Grapevine ... Motown and the California Raisins (1986)

Boys Just Wanna Have

Dance ... *oes It*

for Seth Werner and the fruit of his labors.

"I will probably just do something stupid like have some raisins dancing to 'I Heard It Through the Grapevine.'"[1] And so began what was arguably the most famous use of popular music in an animated advertising commercial of all time. Seth Werner had just arrived at the advertising firm Foote, Cone, & Belding in San Francisco. Werner tells how it happened:

> I have been in advertising, I had been working at an agency in New York, and it was called Marschalk. It was one of the Interpublic companies. We worked on Gillette foamy and Coke Cola products like Sprite, Minute Maid orange soda, things like that. I had done

a campaign for Stroh Beer. It was called Alex the Dog. It was a guy who sent his dog to the refrigerator to get some beers for him; they were all playing poker. You never actually saw the dog do it but you heard the sound effects of the dog opening the refrigerator and he pops off a couple of caps and he pours the beer and then you hear him drinking one. And the guy says something to the effect "Alex you better be drinking your water." I think we had to change the ending two or three times for the networks to approve it. So they didn't think the dog was really drinking beer. So that was actually my first success. That spot took off. It was one of the original Super Bowls spots, people seemed to love it. It actually started to build my career a little bit. So this guy in California, Mike Koelker at Foote, Cone, & Belding in San Francisco hired me. He was some-what famous in his own right. He had done a campaign for Levi's called "The 501 Blues." It was actually an excellent campaign and I thought that it was terrific. It didn't look like any other advertising. It was shot with a long lens, the actors weren't really acting they were just improvising and doing their own thing. It was a pretty cool campaign and so I thought okay this sounds interesting and I picked everything up and I moved to California. I was like 30 years old at the time. So I got there and I had a bit of a career going and when I got there, it seemed like he was responsible for all of the Levi's work and I didn't really have much to do. I would do trade ads or small little things on Levi's. I just felt like this guy collected me the same way he collected watches. He had just wanted to staff up with some people he thought were decent but he really wanted to do all of the good work. So I got a little frustrated that I never got to do anything like Levi's or any of the bigger accounts. So I said to Mike: "You moved me all the way out here to the other coast, can I just have something good to work on. Give me a proj-ect, give me tough assignment." So he said, "Well, we have this one little … it is our smallest account really." They had Levi's and they had Clorox and they had all this big expensive brands that spent a lot of money, and he said, "This is our smallest account. They only spend about five million dollars a year." That may sound like a lot of money but on a national basis, even back in the 80's, that was a pretty small budget. So he said, "The only reason I have a small account like this is to do some good work on it." We had already won a Cleo. Last year we won a Cleo for it, but I don't really like the work and I really want something different and unusual and let's see what you can do. So he said, "That's your baby, go on and take it." I remember that night, that very same night, after he gave me the assignment, I was over a friend's house, over a friend's apartment and they asked me what I was working on. I told them I just got this assignment, it is the California Raisins. I said I would probably just do something stupid like have some raisins dancing to "I Heard It Through the Grapevine." Everybody stopped and for a second I just thought to myself maybe that is not so stupid. I made myself a little note, like I always do, so I remember things the next day and put it in my pocket. Actually, this one I remembered anyway, but I went into work the next day and started talking to my art director and we started plotting it out and that's how it all started to happen. We decided that rather than do it with animation; I had seen the short films done in clay kind of animation. There is a guy named Jimmy Picker out of Brooklyn who had done some pretty cool films. One was called "A Sunday in New York," and it was Mayor Ed Koch singing "New York, New York" on a subway. That was all done in clay animation. He had done one with Jimmy Carter singing, "Georgia on my Mind," and I thought this guy is right up our alley. I called him and he actually said he is too busy to work on it and he couldn't do it. When I called him a second time to do the second one, he regretted having that first phone conversation with me. But at that time he couldn't do it again. So we tracked down this other man name Will Vinton in Portland. He had done a couple of shorts and clay animation as well, and he had actually named it "claymation." He had given it a brand name. So we said, "okay this guy looks good," and he had done a bunch of these but nothing really ever achieved the kind of success we had. He had done like "The Noid" for Pizza Hut. So he said, sure he would love to do this because we were just coming to him and paying him to do it. We started working with him for about six months and put it together.[2]

When asked about the integration of popular music into an animation commercial, Werner said it was different for the times.

> Back then, people were not using music the way they do now. I
> remember back in New York, we were mostly going to people to
> write music for us or write a jingle for us. We would work with
> people in the advertising industry who wrote music. We would
> create mostly original music for things. So that was how you did
> it. I think that there were a couple of people, maybe California
> Cooler, would use some popular songs, but really no one was
> doing that at the time and we had been told in the brief that the
> client really wanted like a celebrity spokesperson. I kind of came
> to them and said the celebrity doesn't have to be a spokesperson,
> the celebrity could be the song and the song is all about who you
> are. Everybody knows that raisins are really dried grapes, and so if
> we talk about California vineyards, we could talk about, we were
> raisins after they were grapes, and try to get that inference across.
> So the whole thing became, "Heard It Through the Grapevine,"
> that's what led us to the whole "Heard It Through the Grape-
> vine," theme for California Raisins. We actually re-wrote some of
> the words, like "raised in the California sunshine," and stuff like
> [Buddy Miles did the vocals] that but really mostly kept the hook
> and used the intro, didn't really use the whole song, we had a lot of
> the intro playing to add mystic. The whole clay animation thing, I
> think, took people by surprise. We had done that just so that they
> would appear real almost, not like it is a cartoon but almost like
> these real little creatures existed. I guess that you can analyze it
> to death but looking back, we were in the right place at the right
> time with the right thing.[3]

Of course, the song was almost as expensive as a celebrity would have
been:

> I believe we spent something like $250,000 for the first year to
> purchase the rights and that was a big expense for them at the time
> but we convinced them that it was actually reasonable especially

if they felt they were going to hire a celebrity and that it would work for them. In fact, we showed them two campaigns at the time and one of them was a celebrity campaign. I had done a second campaign that I also liked and remember that this is the 80's and so the campaign was something like an announcer that comes out and says, "We really can't legally claim that if you have been eating raisins your whole life that you could wind up with the body of say Lonnie Anderson but this woman did," and it is Lonnie Anderson eating raisins. So we did a whole campaign, I think one of them was Walter Mondale, "We can't legally claim you can grow up to be President of the United States if you eat raisins," and he is eating a box of raisins and says, "You can come very very close!" And so we did a whole campaign like that featuring celebrities and raisins and then our other campaign with the dancing raisins and I put on white gloves and danced in front of the raisins board. It was a bunch of farmers basically in Fresno, California and they liked it, they said, "That's it, let's do that." There weren't a lot of groups like that. We were actually before the milk board started doing it. I think maybe there was pork or something like that but basically what they did was they organized all their growers and they made them contribute a tiny percentage of their sales and that became the marketing fund. The idea was to brand the California raisins that were grown there. I think that their competition was from Chile and places like that so they wanted everyone to know that these are from the California growers and we actually kind of make California Raisins a brand because of it.[4]

A little branding, and a little magic.

I think part of the magic of it was that we had a small budget, five million dollars on a national basis does not go very far and so in a way I think people never saw it enough, they got a tease of it but we never had enough budget to have you see it over and over again and get sick of it. So, I think you kind of thought, just enough, or maybe not quite enough and that added to the mystic. There was a company that tracked, and they did this just for themselves actually, to bring notary just to themselves but it was called, "Video Storyboard Tests," was the company and so they track popularity of commercials. They did this for a number of years. They would come out every year with an annual ranking and I think it was either 1986 or 1987, we were ranked as the top commercial in the country. I think it was for two years running actually. The funny part is when you look at our budget, they give the name of the advertiser, and in the budget they have like five million dollars next to us, and the next one below us is Anheiser Busch and they are like eighty million, and then Pepsi and they are at hundred million. All of those big names that you recognize as big advertisers with huge budgets and we are in the single digits.[5]

The commercial was still popular in 1988.

1988 RANK	1987 RANK	BRAND (AGENCY)	ESTIMATED 1988 TV SPENDING (in millions)
		Most Popular Television Commercials of 1988	
1	1	California raisins (Foote, Cone & Belding)	$6.8
2	3	Pepsi/Diet Pepsi (BBDO)	106.4
3	5	McDonald's (Leo Burnett)	385.9
4	2	Bud Light (DDB/Needham)	57.4
5	8	Isuzu (Della Femina, McNamee WCRS)	30.0
6	4	Miller Lite (Backer Spielvogel Bates)	64.5
7	7	Coca-Cola (McCann-Erickson)	68.0
8	—	Stroh's (Lowe Marschalk¹)	18.0
9	12	Wendy's (Backer Spielvogel Bates)	83.5
10	13	Levi's (Foote, Cone & Belding)	37.4
11	18	Partnership for a Drug-Free America (various agencies)	82.5²
12	—	AT&T (N.W. Ayer, Ogilvy & Mather)	216.1
13	—	Johnson's Baby Shampoo (Lintas)	10.0
14	—	Huggies (Ogilvy & Mather)	22.7
15	6	Bartles & Jaymes (Crawford/Wu Films)	26.2
16	—	7-Up (Leo Burnett)	38.5
17	9	Du Pont Stainmaster carpet (BBDO)	29.0
18	11	Jell-O (Young & Rubicam)	30.0
19	—	Nike (Wieden & Kennedy)	16.7
20	—	Michelin (DDB/Needham)	11.8
21	—	Gravy Train (Chiat/Day¹)	6.3
22	—	National Dairy Board (McCann-Erickson)	16.0
23	—	Little Caesar (Cliff Freeman & Partners)	9.9
24	—	Ragu (Waring & LaRosa)	19.1
25	—	King Kuts (J. Walter Thompson)	5.5

¹ Stroh's account has been moved to the Hal Riney & Partners ad agency and Gravy Train account has been switched to the Bayer Bess Vanderwarker agency
² Estimated value of TV time donated for these public-service spots
Sources: Video Storyboard Tests' Commercial Break newsletter and Arbitron's Broadcast Advertisers Reports

In case you haven't *heard*, the song almost didn't happen either. Barry Gordy, the founder of Motown didn't like it at first:

I didn't know this at the time but I recently found out, within the past couple of years, because people have contacted me for the family, but Norman Whitfield wrote it and Norman Whitfield was pretty big force in Motown but no one ever know who he was. He was really kind of behind the scenes, a songwriter and a producer and he wasn't a performer. I think the reality was there was a little bit of a feud between Smokey Robinson and Norman Whitfield. Smokey was Barry's favorite boy and Norman always thought he had more talent and ability. I think that was the reason why, but this was one of his songs. He has a number of others that are famous. He contacted me and had me participate in a couple of Norman Whitfield days. One was in Las Vegas last year and I think they had something in Los Angeles this year. It is funny the family has recently thanked me for helping to bring it back to life because this song was the song and in its day but then raisins just kind of gave it a whole new life.[6]

What role does popular music play in advertising?

I have always thought in everything I do and a lot of the work I have done throughout my career that music has been an important part of it regardless whether it is famous music or not because the best advertising is not a rational appeal. I think the best advertising appeals to people's emotions and then they use the rational part to convince themselves that they are doing the right thing but they are really swayed by their feelings and I think feelings could be a lot stronger than rational thinking. By using music in a lot of the work I have done over the years, I think it just gives color to what we are doing. It gives emotion and feeling to what we are doing. So you are not just hearing the message, you are feeling something that makes you like us. I think that was huge and our mission was to make raisins cool, to make raisins hip and cool. We did as much as we can by untying their shoe laces and putting sun glasses on them and teaching them how to dance but in the end it is the music that truly created the feeling. You can't tell somebody that something is cool; you got to make them feel that. I also feel that it has to be handled right as well. The world is a cynical place and if things are done poorly … I have heard really popular songs be re-recorded and done poorly and it is almost a joke and then people are accused of selling out to do that and you have commercialized yourself and I think it is really also how it is done and keeping the integrity of what you are doing. We tried not to alter it too much when we were doing it.[7]

Final thoughts from Werner …

"I look back on it now, and it kind of just had a life of its own, it took on a life of its own."[8]

The Raisins appeared in "A Claymation Christmas Celebration" singing the Christmas carol, "Rudolph the Red-Nosed Reindeer." It won an Emmy. On November 4, 1988, CBS aired a primetime special entitled Meet the Raisins! A sequel aired in 1990 under the title "Raisins: Sold Out!" The Raisins were the official mascots of Post Raisin Bran, appearing in commercials and on packaging. Raisins merchandise in the Smithsonian Institution. Hardee's restaurant offered Raisins as part of a promotion for their Cinnamon 'N' Raisin biscuits. A Raisins Fan Club began in 1987. There's even a Raisins website devoted just to all things raisins (see www.californiaraisins.com). And *Entertainment Weekly* named The Raisins one of "The 50 Best Commercials of All Time."[9]

1. "The celebrity could be the song and the song is all about who you are." Seth Werner
2. "Music gives color to what we are doing. It gives emotion and feeling to what we are doing. So you are not just hearing the message, you are feeling something that makes you like us." Seth Werner

California Raisins Commercial Lyrics

I heard it through the grapevine

Raised in the California Sunshine

Don'tcha know I heard it through the grapevine ...

CHAPTER 4

"Revolution" … The Beatles and Nike (1987)

In 1987, sneaker manufacturer Nike had passed the $1 billion mark in corporate sales. However, its chief competitor at the time, Reebok, was the world's No. 1 sneaker company. Nike was then in the process of revamping its advertising and marketing strategies and had already hooked up with a rising NBA basketball star named Michael Jordan. The company had also come up with a tag line for promoting a new group of Nike Air athletic shoes—"Revolution in Motion." But this campaign needed some catchy music to use in its TV advertising to help launch the shoe. That's when Nike and its advertising agency, Weiden & Kennedy, got the idea of using the Beatles' classic 1960s' song, "Revolution" to help sell the shoes. However, Beatles' music—at least in its original form as sung by the Beatles themselves—had never been used in a TV commercial before. In one case in 1985 the Beatles' song "Help!" was used in a Lincoln-Mercury car ad, but the song was performed in that case by a sound-alike group. Nike's ad agency, Weiden & Kennedy, wanted the real thing. "We never considered sound-alikes," said the agency's Kelley Stoutt, explaining Nike's intentions for its "revolution" ad to *Time* magazine in May 1987. "In our minds," said Stoutt, emphasizing the plan to use the original song, "it was the Beatles or no one." In mid-1987, Nike made a deal to use the Beatles song in their ad campaign shelling out $500,000 to do so. However, Nike didn't make the deal with the Beatles, but rather, with pop star Michael Jackson and EMI-Capitol Records. According to *Time*, Nike paid $250,000 to the record companies and a similar amount to Jackson to use the song for one year. Jackson had acquired "Revolution" and 200 other Beatles tunes in 1985 when he paid $47.5 million to an Australian group for a catalog of some 4,000 songs, including the Beatles' songs. The Beatles, however, along with their record label, Apple, had decided after the earlier use of "Help!" in the 1985 Ford Lincoln-Mercury ad, that there would be no more use of Beatles music in advertising. Yet the Beatles didn't own the rights to "Revolution" any longer; and Nike had paid its fee to Jackson and Capitol Records for the right to use the song .... Music publishing rights in the early 1960s were valued somewhat differently, and many performers didn't always realize the full economic value of their songs. The Beatles, for their part, had also made a few management mistakes along the way, and were not well served by some of their business partners and managers. With the right advice at the time, the Beatles might as well have retained full and clear control of "Revolution" and their other early songs. Still, there is much more to this story than space permits here. In any case, by early 1987, Nike believed it had the legal rights to use "Revolution," and proceeded to make the ad with the original Beatles music. The ad began running on television in mid-March 1987. Then, in the summer of 1987, the three surviving Beatles along with their record label, Apple, filed a lawsuit objecting to Nike's use of the song. The suit was aimed at Nike, its ad agency, Wieden & Kennedy, and Capitol-EMI Records. The TV ad with the music—and there were at least four versions—continued to run as the litigation proceeded. "Revolution" was written by John Lennon in the spring of 1968, then a tumultuous time in the U.S. and Europe. Vietnam War protests and other civil unrest had occurred. In Paris that May, about the time Lennon wrote the song, student demonstrations had reached a fevered pitch. A massive strike there and resulting riots led to the collapse of the government of Charles DeGaulle. Lennon aimed his song at the world's young revolutionaries, agreeing with their basic beliefs but advocating non-violence. The song, which became the Beatles first venture into political territory, was recorded in July 1968 at Abbey Road studios in London. It was released on B-side of the "Hey

Jude" single in August that year. The single reached No. 12 on the
U.S. music charts. The song was a product of the recording ses-
sions for the Beatle's *White Album*, and in fact, the original slower
version of "Revolution," sometimes called "Revolution 1," appears
on that album. The Nike ads that ran using the "Revolution"
music, however, were well received by many who saw them. One
of the ads—showing a collage of quick-cut sports scenes that fit
well with the music—was generally upbeat and energetic. It was
purposely crafted by the producers to have the look of a grainy
black-and- white home movie. They wanted the ad to come across
as "a kind of radical sports documentary," and in 1987–88, it
likely had that effect. It showed a few quick clips of professional,
well-known athletes—including very brief appearances of John
McEnroe and Michael Jordan. But there were also lots of shots of
amateurs doing their own sports things—from joggers and tennis
players, to toddlers, rope skippers, and air guitarists. Some Madison Avenue managers at the time thought it was a coup for Nike
to have used original Beatles' music in the spot, calling the music
"a very, very powerful tool." Others weren't so sure, pointing to the
antiwar demonstrations of the Vietnam War era when the song
was first aired, suggesting that association might be the more powerful one. Meanwhile, as the litigation over the use of the music
dragged on, Nike continued to air the ad. At least four versions of
the TV spot were produced and run, including one version with
women joggers. But finally, in March 1988, although the case was
still in court, Nike decided to discontinue airing the ads using the
"Revolution" song. More than a year later, in November 1989 the
Los Angeles Daily News reported that the "tangle of lawsuits
between the Beatles and their American and British record companies has been settled." One condition of the out-of-court settlement was that terms of the agreement would be kept secret. The
settlement was reached among the three groups of interests
involved: the former surviving Beatles—George Harrison, Paul
McCartney, and Ringo Starr—John Lennon's wife, Yoko Ono;
and the music businesses, Apple, EMI, and Capitol Records.
A spokesman for Yoko Ono noted of the lawsuit and settlement,

however, It's such a confusing myriad of issues that even people who have been close to the principals have a difficult time grasping it. Attorneys on both sides of the Atlantic have probably put their children through college on this. Turns out that the Nike "Revolution" ad not only helped to sell lots of Nike athletic shoes, but also helped to sell, re-energize, and introduce the Beatles' music to a whole new generation of listeners. In fact, according to one blogger who was in high school at that time, Nike's ad helped introduce him and his peers to the Beatles' music. "As a kid entering high school and discovering music, hearing 'Revolution' every night on TV opened my eyes and ears to the whole world of Beatles music," he writes at his blog, *dsicle.com.* "Suddenly, the Beatles weren't just dusty records on my parent's shelf, they were current, *popular* musicians." He adds that in 1987 there were certain songs guaranteed to be played at every high school party, including: "Fight For Your Right" by the Beastie Boys, "It's Tricky" by RUN-DMC, "Lean On Me" by Club Nouveau—and also "Revolution" by the Beatles. "As amazing as it sounds," he writes, "a 20 year-old Beatles song was popular with high school kids—no doubt spurred by the Nike Air Max 'Revolution' commercial." During the summer of 1987, the Beatles' *White Album*, which contained a version of "Revolution," was released on CD for the first time, reaching No. 18 on the *Billboard* albums chart nearly 20 years after its original release. In the advertising world, meanwhile, the Nike "Revolution" ad was given high marks, seen as an excellent example of how advertising and iconic music can help with "branding" a product, elevating it in the minds of consumers, and distinguishing it from its competitors. Some advertising wags even say the 60-second ad played an important role in creating the Nike brand. The ad's mixture of famous athletes like Michael Jordan and John McEnroe with everyday, average-person joggers and weekend athletes also had a pointed effect, as author John Katz observes in his 1994 book on Nike, *Just Do It*: The message seemed designed to diminish the distance between the greatest athletes and people who play and exercise for fun. Though Nike dogma would have previously precluded the potential muddying of a great athlete's image, the carefully contrived commercial ennobled every kid, pro athlete, and duffer who appeared. With the Beatles in the background, the commercial was like a sixty second celebration. And the shoes moved out of the stores. Indeed, the Beatles' music, mixed with the powerful sports images, helped give this ad an emotional tone and power, as marketing consultant Tim Glowa observed in 2004: "This commercial illustrates how television advertising can become the ultimate emotion builder... and demonstrates that a brand can be emotional and thought provoking. Like the use of other rock tunes in advertising, Nike's "Revolution" ad and the litigation that followed, further pushed the envelope on the use of popular music in advertising." "The Nike 'Revolution' use was monumental in many ways," explained Josh Rabinowitz, director of music at the Grey Group in a 2009 *Ad Week* piece. Not only did the ad "resonate with the visuals and concept," said Rabinowitz, it also "really opened the door to high-concept ads utilizing great – and expensive – music." Nike's Revolution ad also broke ground for "a cottage industry of commercial music-licensing experts and internal commercial-licensing resources," according to Rabinowitz. In fact, entire departments in those specializations were created at record labels and music publishers, "because nobody wanted to get embroiled in that type of legal nuisance again."[1]

If any publicity is good publicity the campaign was great. *The New York Times* reported:

Nike Inc., the company that used the original recording of the Beatles' "Revolution" in an advertisement for running shoes, said yesterday that a $15 million suit filed by the Beatles' British and American companies was groundless. Philip H. Knight, chairman of Nike, was responding to the suit filed by Apple Corps Ltd. and Apple Records in State Supreme Court in Manhattan last week against Nike; Wieden & Kennedy Advertising, the company hired by Nike to produce the commercials, and Capitol-E.M.I. Records. Mr. Knight said the suit was only "the latest skirmish" in a legal battle between Apple and Capitol-E.M.I. "We negotiated and paid for all legal rights from Capitol-E.M.I., which has the licensing rights to all the Beatles' original recordings, and S.B.K., which represents Michael Jackson's interests as owner of the publishing rights," Mr. Knight said. "Any implication that we did anything improper or disrespectful to the Beatles is untrue in our opinion." The commercials edit the three-minute John Lennon-Paul McCartney song into 30-second and 60-second versions. The advertisements began running in mid-March and have now tapered off, Mr. Knight said, but he expects new versions using "Revolution" to run in the fall. Leonard M. Marks, Apple's lawyer, said that Apple had offered to drop the suit if the commercials were withdrawn. Melissa Schumer, a Nike spokesman, said the company was unaware of that offer. Yoko Ono, John Lennon's widow, expressed approval when the commercial was released; she was quoted in *Time* magazine as saying the commercial "is making John's music accessible to a new generation." The surviving ex-Beatles have not commented publicly. Leonard M. Marks, Apple's lawyer, said yesterday that Ms. Ono and the three surviving Beatles each own 25 percent of Apple and that the company requires "unanimity among the four Beatles' interests in order to act," implying that Ms. Ono had concurred in bringing the suit. "They are all outraged about the commercial," he said. Beatles Received Nothing. Mr. Marks said that Nike had paid $250,000 for the rights to the recording (which a Capitol spokesman would not confirm or dispute) and that the Beatles received no payments for the commercial. In a statement, Bob O'Neill, general counsel and vice president of Capitol-E.M.I., called the suit "absurd and nonsensical." Recordings carry two copyrights, for publishing (the words and music of a song) and for performance, as embodied in the recording. The Nike suit brings to three the number of lawsuits now pending over ownership of Beatles recordings and royalties on them. In July, Apple filed a $40 million suit in Manhattan charging that Capitol-E.M.I. unfairly delayed release of the Beatles' albums on compact disks for two years and was charging too much for packaging costs. A suit filed in 1979 charges that Capitol-E.M.I. underpaid the Beatles for their recording royalties between 1969 and 1979. The amount under contention was recently reduced by a court in Manhattan from $80 million to $30 million, and allegations of fraud were dropped. "It's now a contractual dispute," said Sue Satriano, a Capitol spokesman. [2]

Even TheStreet.com voted it #97 on their "The Basics of Business History: 100 Events That Shaped a Century" saying:

It's not the first time the ideals of the 1960s—freedom, individuality, antimaterialism, dissent—are called upon to push product. But it may stand as the biggest co-optation. Right at the height of the Summer of Love anniversary celebration, Nike (NKE_) uses the Beatles song to sell sneakers. Now it's almost impossible to escape ads that sell not just products but breaking the rules, dude.[3]

But how did George and Paul and their record label feel about it?
"The Beatles position is that they don't sing jingles to peddle sneakers, beer, pantyhose or anything else. ... They wrote and recorded these songs as artists and not as pitch men for any product." (Apple, July 1987)

If it's allowed to happen, every Beatles song ever recorded is going to be advertising women's underwear and sausages. We've got to put a stop to it in order to set a precedent. Otherwise it's going to be a free-for-all. It's one thing when you're dead, but we're still around! They don't have any respect for the fact that we wrote and recorded those songs, and it was our lives. (George Harrison, November 1987)

The most difficult question is whether you should use songs for commercials. I haven't made up my mind. Generally, I don't like it, particularly with the Beatles stuff. When twenty years have passed maybe we'll move into the realm where it's okay to do it. (Paul McCartney, February 1988)

1. Unless you are looking for publicity, make sure the band is on board.
2. A popular music in advertising campaign shouldn't cause a Revolution.

CHAPTER 5

"Be My Baby" ... The Ronettes and Levi's (1989)

What do you get when you combine a great song with a pair of jeans? Excellence.

In 1989, Levi's, the jeans company, used the Ronettes' classic 1963 song "Be My Baby" as background music for a TV ad. Ad story: A good Samaritan in the middle of nowhere, pulls his pick-up truck over to the side of the road to help a distressed driver tow his overheated car to town for a repair. The driver and his lady friend date are well-dressed, presumably heading out for dinner or a show. The subplot in this tale, however, is the instant chemistry and eye contact going on between the Good Samaritan and the distressed driver's lady companion. A towing fix is made by the Good Samaritan who sheds his 501 Levi jeans to make a jerry-rigged towing line with the distressed car. The lady, meanwhile, is beckoned by the Good Samaritan to ride along with him in the front seat of his truck on the ride to town. The jerry-rigged, Levi's towing line, however, "unfortunately" gives out on the way to town, setting the distressed car and its driver adrift, as the Good Samaritan and his new lady friend ride off into the sunset .... The ad's fade-out tagline: "Levis 501: Separates The Men From The Boys."[1]

It's all about the song...

It was one of the defining rock 'n' roll songs of the 1960s – a song notable for its role in advancing a new sound that changed pop music – is the Ronettes' 1963 blockbuster, "Be My Baby." It was sung by three young girls from New York's Spanish Harlem

who came be known as the Ronettes – sisters Estelle and Ronnie
Bennett, and their cousin, Nedra Talley. In 2006, the U.S. Library
of Congress chose the Ronettes' "Be My Baby" to be added to the
National Recording Registry. The song is also ranked at No. 22 on
Rolling Stone's list of "The 500 Greatest Songs of All Time" published in 2004. Brian Wilson of the Beach Boys – no slouch when
it came to composing ground-breaking 1960s' music of his own –
has called "Be My Baby" one of the greatest pop records ever made
and is his "all-time favorite song." Wilson was in his car when he
first heard the tune on the radio, and being the composer and
arranger that he was, stopped the car to give the song a closer listen. "I had to pull off the road," he said. "I couldn't believe it. The
choruses blew me away ..." Wilson, in fact, wrote a famous Beach
Boys song, "Don't Worry Baby," initially as a follow-up intended
for the Ronettes, but it was turned down for that purpose.[2]

Len Peltier is the former vice president and global creative director at
Levi's. He started his career in advertising at A&M Records as an associ-
ate creative director. He has won a Grammy and been nominated twice.
"Imaging a product or brand and keeping it on target is almost identical
to guiding the career and image of an artist,"[3] he has said. When asked
what song best described Levi's, he said:

> The music at our last editor event really captured the Levi spirit.
> We brought in a group of teenage cellists that I ran into one night
> in San Francisco, who played everything from Bach to Lady Gaga.
> These 19-year-olds, who were trained at the conservatory, we're
> playing pop music through a refined, classical lens—that's what
> Levi's is about right now.[4]

Although Peltier was not at Levi's at the time of this ad, he did provide
great insight into the Levi's commercial philosophy:

> In that particular period, and it's very cyclier, it was a story tell-
> ing device for sure. [This] one in particular obviously points at a
> situation on some kind of a rye way or creates a story, it seems to

have then shifted into something more emphatic where it was just to create emotion so you would have some bit crash and beautiful montage but it wasn't saying as much. That particular period was very interesting because there were stories. It is interesting how the audience has changed as they've grown up and seen and listened to different music up through MTV, and just the evolution. The artist used to think if it were a big campaign, this was very cool. If it were too commercial, you were a sellout. Now artists are dying to get in commercials. It is not a sellout anymore. There is some pretty amazing stuff being done but that period in particular was really about story telling. Pop culture was definitely the moment. I mean back then during "501 Blues," which was more of a jingle, music was in the forefront in a way that it really hadn't been before commercially and so that stuff was probably considered very edgy back then, if I remember correctly. I was in advertising then, and I would collect Levi's commercials even though I wasn't working there because they always had a really interesting use of music and in Europe they would go a little bit stronger with kind of the edge of the story telling in a way they were almost hyper-realizing Americana which is very interesting because it had such a fun fantasy. [In the case of this ad] it is funny because you could say it is dated and it is timeless at the same time. It is a classic, guy gets girl, and it is rye which I think is very much in the Levi sensibility. It puts a power in the woman's position too of making a different choice, which is interesting for that time period, which is a little forward for what was going on in most women's advertising back then. But I think mostly it is super playful. It is going to be that guy that you always aspire to be, getting the girl, being creative and being bold. The brand is always about being bold and taking risks and that's what it was founded on, for God's sake, but it became a very, not sensualized but sensual kind of sexy, guy gets girl thing. I love the ones also where she is always stealing his pants became a gigantic trend, boyfriend's jeans, which is based on girls stealing their boyfriend's 501s. So I think that was kind of a classic storyline and, of course, playing with the whole idea of telling it, being one of the iconic logos stretching or testing the strength of the jeans in different directions and kind of using that to play back the heritage without being dusty or kind of old fashion about it. It was also being real cleaver. And I don't even know if everyone back then even knew that, that logo, they must if you have ever had a pair but if you notice on the back patch representing the strength and quality of the product. Kind of where you can textualizing in this kind of rye way. So it is kind of fun all the way round. It tells the story about the brand and it points at the heritage a little bit. It is definitely kind of classic storytelling but then the song really sets it off into a different mood. It does have a lot of the great elements of a classic commercial. I would guess that the ad was written around that song.[5]

When asked about the use of popular music in advertising in general, Peltier was a big fan:

I think at times it is almost the easy way in, in that it is always an emotional response. It connects to a time and culture. I think it is most interesting when it's time left, if it is a classic song that really somehow sustains, it is always stronger. It is always going to create emotion, it is always going to connect the viewers to something. It is not always the most conceptual way to go when you do any kind of an endemic spot but does almost fit you more strongly. We have gone in different directions, and like I said, we tried some really interesting things with poems and with recordings like that and it is just a totally different mood and it hits you a different way and I think that the reason for that too is that consumers are used to hearing and seeing things done a certain way and in that particular spot it is very much tied to the storytelling. You think it lasts. It kind of really bonds but there is always an emotional reaction and that is what it is about. Sometimes we will do an inspirational film about the whole kind of path that the brand and you bring it up to the contemporary and whenever you set that to something that really rocks the crowd or connects with them, you get an emotional response, there is a lot of territory. It definitely triggers something in you and sometimes it is nostalgic and sometimes not. If you ask a lot of people at [Levi's], what it does connect with, they will go back to rock and roll. They will go back to I would say Springsteen or San Francisco. For me, if I came up at a certain time, it is definitely punk in down town New York, that was such a moment for Levi's. There were those and I think the other thing is it is chosen by those artists. It is not something that we sell to them. The brand is adopted by artists because of the freedom that the jeans represent and the stories that they tell and so there is such a strong connection. We did a thing with Patty Smith and I got to photograph her and she gave me her oldest pair of 501s, as a gift for the archives, which was pretty incredible, thinking about the shows that those have been in and the people they have known. And so there is definitely a relationship with music that goes deeper than just using music to tell a story. These are friendships and people do it because they believe in the brand and the story of the brand. So that is pretty rare, that is a gift. You can't get a lot of brands without paying somebody to do it and luckily we always get to do that, which is pretty nice.[6]

When asked where he thought music and advertising was going, Peltier said,

This is just my opinion, the audiences change so much, jingles don't work because they are telling you what to think about some-thing, unless it is ironic. I could see it being done ironically, that is just a different time where people were kind of told to buy stuff or they used it to kind of like you burn it into memory and kids especially are so much more sophisticated and they have seen everything and heard everything. Popular music will never, I don't think, ever be out of it. I mean it is being used differently to tell a story. I think sound design is an incredibly powerful. A lot of artists are getting into doing that stuff, not just licensing a song. But I think pop music will always be part of it. It is just coming in different ways, in more unusual ways. You see artists connecting with brands, but I think brands are also getting smart enough to use artists where it is not just seeing something to say Rihanna is wearing our product. That is not really connecting with your audience but doing the project with Rihanna as a brand to do something good or a music program or something for kids or something creative, that is kind of how it is getting more into the mainstream. So it is doing a little more than just buying a song. That seems like the easy way out.[7]

1. "Imaging a product or brand and keeping it on target is almost identical to guiding the career and image of an artist." Len Peltier
2. "We're playing pop music through a refined, classical lens." Len Peltier
3. "Music is a story telling device. It is always going to create emotion. It is always going to connect the viewers to something. " Len Peltier

Levi's Commercial

Be my little baby
(My one and only baby)
Say you'll be my darlin'
(Be my, be my baby)
Levi's 501 … Separates the Men from the Boys

CHAPTER 6

"Like A Rock" ... Bob Seger and Chevy (1991)

"Like a Rock" was written by Bob Seger, recorded with The Silver Bullet Band, and released in May 1986 as the second single and title cut from album of the same name. It made it to No. 1 on the Billboard Mainstream Rock Tracks. "'Like a Rock' was inspired partly by the end of a relationship I had that had lasted for 11 years," Seger said.

> You wonder where all that time went. But beyond that, it expresses my feeling that the best years of your life are in your late teens when you have no special commitments and no career. It's your last blast of fun before heading into the cruel world.[1]

The story could have begun and ended there. If not for the fact that "Like A Rock," for over 10 years, was used in Chevrolet truck commercials. It was one of the longest-running advertising campaigns in history (and was also featured in the film *The Weather Man*, starring Nicolas Cage and Michael Caine). It began in 1991 and lasted until 2004. The father of the Chevy "Like A Rock" campaign was Donald Gould, a longtime Campbell-Ewald agency who died in 1998.[2]

Kurt Ritter was marketing manager of Chevrolet trucks from 1991 to 1995. He said then, "'I thought 'Like a Rock' was over the moon, it captured the physicality of the truck,' the independence of the truck buyer and the vehicle's durability." A fundamental obstacle was persuading Seger to give permission to use the song. Initially he refused, not wanting it to be used in a commercial. After trying to persuade Seger's manager, Punch Andrews, for four months, the call from Andrews agreeing to use the song in return for creative input on all the commercials finally came. What had changed? Seger was in a bar in Detroit when someone asked him, "When are you going to do something for the auto workers?"[3]

Ritter is now CEO of Saatchi & Saatchi's Los Angeles office and of Team One, after spending 32 years at Chevrolet. He was marketing manager of Chevrolet trucks from 1991 to 1995. He remembers it well:

> Well, I was brought in to be a marketing director for Chevy Trucks. I remember going to the airport to catch a plane and they had just announced that we were just dropping the first bombs on Bagdad so I think it was probably February of '91, in that timeframe, it was spring, and the state of shipping trucks was not very good. The state of the advertising in the category was much mudslinging outrageously dumb product comparison between Ford and Chevy that were not spiraling, didn't really tell a good product story and weren't building brands in the process. They were actually destructive to the brands because they were just taking cheapshots at each other. So in order to do something that was more uplifting than was out there in the category at the time. ... So that is like February or March when I go down on site, it caused for repositioning Chevy trucks. We went out and we interviewed any number of stakeholders from the people in our product planning staff about what was coming in the pipeline to engineers that worked on the product, even some older retired people that had a hand in past Chevy truck stuff. What we learned was that we were not the fastest trucks, we were not the most technologically advanced trucks at all but we did one redeeming thing really really well and that is our trucks really lasted a long long time. We could prove that statistically and we could also look into the product pipeline and understand that we were getting even better as time

went by. So what makes you really proud when you go home at night with your family and the Dodge breaks down and the Ford breaks down and the Chevy keeps going. So we knew that we were that and so we came in with a team, market research with focus groups and so forth. We came up with a positioning which was pretty simple; it was Chevy trucks are dependable and long lasting. So we felt pretty comfortable about that line of products that got us to the point that even knowing the future would have been pretty comfortable. It was not that overly aspirational thing to our current customer base or others to believe us, that was attractive to us and it was attractive to others that had never tried us before. So we now have to come up with a campaign that communicated that position and panel came forth with a written (inaudible) that puts some images together on a sound track, like a rap. It was sort of instant inspiration to me. Later you always have different questions that you'll either ask yourself or try to anticipate your management asking you but I do remember instantly thinking that was really wonderful stuff that would communicate our position. I learned then and I have used for many years something equal to that but brief marketing stuff doesn't invent the truth that tries to discover a truth and tell that truth in a very compelling way. The agency liked it from the standpoint that it captured the physicality of trucks and there were many lyrics that we could use in the song over time. Some of the other questions after the initial inspirational—were women going to like this. So we had to research on that specifically and it was like instantly winning ... it like reflected the their spirit as well in terms of they liked to be considered like a lot. They liked to be in dependable to their families, to friends and to their husbands. So it worked on that level too. There wasn't a problem at all with women; in fact it probably represented a lot of what they believe in themselves or would like to be. So I've rambled a lot but that is kind of how we got to that stage of getting Bob Seger and Punch Andrews to sign off on a song that was a journey to get them to do that. Bob had not done that before and he was getting a lot of pressure from his contemporaries and they tried elsewhere not to sell out, not to sell the song and our interest was more in a more fundamental sound than the song done what maybe the case with other marketers where they are interested in a break through jingle. We weren't interested in that. We were interested in something that captured the soul of the brand and would be around for a long time but I think there were some pressures from I don't want to be selling out. I don't want to lose creative control and so we had to give creative control to Punch Andrews who I got to know very well over the years and honestly really liked the guy and understood his role and he was a guy that really believed in the campaign too so it was a plus on that side but early on they didn't know our intentions, they kind of sure didn't trust us with that but over time we earned their trust as well to do the song. So we eventually got them to sign in August and really did have a backup campaign. We were running short of time for sure because football season was right around the corner. We had trucks that were going to be produced but finally got it. I remember the story that I think Don told me it and Punch verified it that Seger was in a saloon in Detroit and some factory worker came up to him. Car sales lingered and so there's a lot of workers laid off and he saw Bob Seger and said, "Bob, what have you ever done to help this town? What have you ever done to help the automotive factory workers that come to your concerts over the years?" Later he accused us of planting that when we didn't but I am told that was put Bob and Punch forward to go ahead and sign up with us at the time. So we had all of our words already to go because we didn't have a backup campaign and that is how it happened.[4]

Seger never said whether he liked the campaign or not but he stopped performing the song in concerts until 2013.

We haven't done it for 27 years, so it's like a new song for us live. Once people recognize the song we're playing, it starts out really

really quiet. And once I sing the first line it gets a big response, so it's a lot of fun.[5]

Seger said the reason why the song took so long to get back in rotation on tour was because he didn't have the right combination of band members to perform it the way he wanted to. The song is nearly six minutes long and was part of Chevrolet's truck campaign advertising for more than a decade. "Part of the problem (with not playing 'Like a Rock' for so long) was that Rick Zito took off for Fleetwood Mac and we could never find anybody who could play it very well," Seger said,

> And our new guitar player, Rob McNelly from Nashville, really just nails it and it's unusual. So we just didn't do it (until the band members were in place). It's a really long song, too, about six minutes, and we had to find a spot for it. It fits good in the set now.[6]

1. "Song must communicate brand's position." Kurt Ritter
2. "Song must have more than one line to use if you expect to use it over a period of time." Kurt Ritter
3. Doesn't hurt to have a little "help" from a fan of the artist.

Chevrolet Trucks—Commercial Copy

America is still the land of rugged individualists
Like a rock ... I'm as strong as I can be
Like a rock ... Nothing ever got to me
And everyone of them demands something different from their Chevy
    truck but they all want the same thing

Like a rock …

The most dependable, long-lasting trucks on the road

Like a rock …

CHAPTER 7

"Start Me Up" ... The Rolling Stones and Microsoft (1995)

Who can forget that guitar? As soon as it *started* you knew it was the Rolling Stones. And who can forget the first time you *started* Windows? What two things do they have in common? Mick Jagger and Bill Gates, of course. The year is 1995. Microsoft was about to launch Windows 95 and *out of the clear blue sky*[1] Wieden & Kennedy (Microsoft's advertising agency) proposes to then Chief Operating Officer, Bob Herbold, an idea. "The $200 million Windows 95 campaign was the first grand celebration of the Microsoft name, Herbold said."[2] When it was done, the name recognition of Microsoft as a software company had gone from 4 percent in 1994 to 70 percent in 1996.[3] What follows is excerpt from an interview with the *Puget Sound Business Journal*.[4]

Bob: *So I went in to Bill and said "Well, we got this piece of advertising that we really like for Windows 95" and everybody in the company is working on some aspect of Windows 95. This was a "bet the farm" project at Microsoft and Bill's reaction was "Well, what's the cost?" I want to use this fancy music and I said, "Well, it is pretty expensive." I said, "Before we get into that, we have an Executive Group Meeting coming up where the top thirty or so people in the company would get together once a month, all of the VP's and above and at that point we only had 25 or so VP's." I said, "I want to show this ad to get their reaction and see how they react and then we can talk whether we want to go ahead."*

Interviewer: So you didn't give them a figure?

Bob: *No, and so we get in there and naturally half of these people around the table are sales people, very enthusiastic, and so cranked up the music, showed the storyboard. We actually had the agency make a rough of the commercial. What that constitutes is you're seeing pictures not live characters; you are seeing pictures but the music is there. So we played this 60 second commercial in its rough form and they went wild because the music is sensational, as everybody knows. So wow enthusiasm! So I go back the next day, it seems like the troops like it really understand this is exciting. He said, "Well, what is it in terms of cost?" I said, "I think it is going to cost $3 to $3.5 for million to sign this thing for six months" and he about fell off his chair. He said, "Well, where are you going to get that money?" I said something to the equivalent of 'from you' but in a more cordial way, I am sure. I don't recall exactly but anyway to make a long story short, he was enthused about it also. So eventually he said, "Go work them over; get the price down." "We are going to work Mick Jagger over!!!" I said, "You understand that I just found out that they have never licensed a piece of their music, any music, for a television commercial; this is the first time." Because this product is exciting with what is going on with the world and technology. "Oh, that's nice." Emotionally that was somewhat of support from him. So anyway we ended up making the deal and we paid a lot money for that.*

Interviewer: Did you get the price down?

Bob: *No, well, that part, we got down to about three.*

Herbold had been recruited from Proctor & Gamble where he was senior vice president of Advertising and Information Services. He has a bachelor of science in mathematics from the University of Cincinnati and both a master's degree in mathematics and a PhD in computer science from Case Western Reserve University. When asked what makes popular music in advertising excellent in general, and about the Windows 95 campaign specifically, he said,

Even my experience at Proctor Gamble where I was very involved with marketing, especially the last several years, where I was the Senior VP with marketing reporting to me. I had seen music work well if it was a good match and so I think this one was particularly good since we were interested in publicizing the start button on the new Windows 95 screen. Everything starts as far as Windows 95 goes with the start button. This was a natural. It was why Wieden and Kennedy proposed it, was a very interesting match up to the product. If it is going to work, it's got to have a good match to the product and be sensible in the context that the message and so I am sure that in the future there will be some of it. I don't think it will grow, I don't think it will decline; I think it plays a role. It is one of many different approaches that can be used but there is nothing that is going to make it more popular or less popular. In fact, given the web, it is harder to pull off music related advertising, just like it is harder and harder to pull off testimonial advertising in the context of a fleeting moment. It is all online compared to the traditional television advertising which is fast becoming a relic of the past.[5]

1. "Music works well if it was a good match." Bob Herbold
2. "Be sensible in the context with the message." Bob Herbold
3. "Music plays a role." Bob Herbold

CHAPTER 8

"Desert Rose" ... Sting and Jaguar (1999)

Is it a Sting commercial or a Jaguar commercial? Does the Brand in the album Brand New Day stand for Jaguar or Sting? The fact that the answer to both of these questions is not totally clear could be the reason why it clearly worked ... .

The year is 1999. It's fall. Sting has a new album. It's called *Brand New Day*. Sting feels good about the record. "I feel the millennium is very much a part of this record—and as my strategy in life is to be optimistic, in art I want to be the same."[1] The first single, the title cut *Brand New Day*, receives a chilly radio reception (although it eventually became the theme song for CBS' *The Early Show* from 1999 to 2000) with only a handful of stations playing it. As Miles Copeland, his manager at the time, tells it: "the album was doing fine but it was stopped at 900,000 but the single. Sting was no longer a Top 40 artist; MTV didn't even play the video."[2] Not all that surprising considering his previous studio album *Mercury Falling* failed to produce a radio hit. But Sting is used to having hits. Lots of hits.

Born Gordon Matthew Thomas Sumner on October 2, 1951, in Wallsend, United Kingdom. Renamed *Sting* by a fellow in Phoenix

Photo By: Kevin Mazur

Jazzmen (because of the black and yellow striped sweater). As a member of The Police or solo, Sting has received 16 Grammy Awards beginning in 1981, a Golden Globe, an Emmy Award, and several Oscar nominations for Best Original Song. He is a member of both the Rock and Roll and the Songwriters Halls of Fame. He started as a school teacher by day and a bass player at night with bands like the Newcastle Big Bands, the Jazzmen, Earthrise, and Last Exit. It was with Last Exit that Stewart Copeland, a drummer with another band Curved Air, saw him and the two formed The Police eventually adding Andy Summers and Stewart's brother Copeland as their manager. With "Roxanne" in hand, they signed with A&M Records. When "Roxanne" was not embraced in London, The Police went to America and began to successfully tour. The band returned to the UK to find the reissued "Roxanne" single charting, and began to sellout venues. The debut album *Outlandos d'Amour* (1978) delivered hits with "Roxanne," "Can't Stand Losing You," and "So Lonely" followed by *Reggatta de Blanc* (October, 1979) with "Message in the Bottle" and "Walking On The Moon." More hit albums would follow with *Zenyatta Mondatta* (1980) featuring "Don't Stand So Close To Me" and "De Do Do Do, De Da Da Da;" *Ghost In The Machine* (1981) with "Every Little Thing She Does Is Magic," "Invisible Sun," and "Spirits In the Material World," *Synchronicity* (1983) with "Every Breath You Take," "Wrapped Around Your Finger," "King of Pain," and "Synchronicity II." In 1984,

The Police broke up and Sting went solo with each new album a bit more eclectic than the one before beginning with *The Dream Of The Blue Turtles*, but still producing occasional hits like "If You Love Somebody." Over the next decade and a half, Sting did various albums solidifying his solo career winning Grammys and adding movie and Broadway acting roles. But it had been awhile since he had a big hit, and in the music business, every day is a new day with little regard to what you have done rather what have you done lately.

The choice of a second single was crucial. Copeland wanted "Desert Rose" to be first single but the record company chose "Brand New Day." Now "the Europeans wanted 'Desert Rose,' and everybody thought that single would work for them but not in America," admitted Copeland. So, when "Desert Rose" was getting ready to be released, and the first song had failed to lead the way, there was a new sense of urgency. Still, Sting refused to be predictable when he put *Desert Rose* on the album. He loved it and wanted others to love it. "'Desert Rose' is a song I care passionately about," said Sting. "[I]t's a duet between an Arab singer and a Western singer and it has a political message, if you like, along with a musical one."[3] The Arab singer was Cheb Mami and he and Sting seemed to be on the same page. "The song," Sting comments,

> is about longing ... sexual longing, romantic longing, within a larger concept, which is philosophical longing for meaning or God or whatever. I asked Cheb Mami (Algerian singing sensation) to compose Arabic lyrics. I gave him the counter-melody, but didn't tell him what the song was about. He came back a few days later and started to sing. When I said "what are you singing about" he replied, "longing." I said, "well, it's very strange you should say that." But it does prove my theory that the music was writing the songs.[4]

The reaction from radio was the same as for the first single. Maybe a video would help. The creative involved a Desert, of course, with Sting driving to a concert. In a car. But what car? The video's director Paul Boyd gave Sting some options. "I chose the Jaguar S-Type. It's a beautiful car and it evoked the feeling of style we were trying to achieve."[5] The story might have ended there if not for Miles Copeland. He knew the music promotion business well. Coming off *Brand New Day*, he knew the budget would be tight and impatient. "The label had earmarked $1.8 million to market the single," Copeland said, "including $800,000 to make the video."[6] He saw the video and the plan became clear. "My God, it's a car commercial."[7] He knew that automobile manufacturers had big budgets—eight to 10 times what had been allocated. So he called a few people and found that Jaguar was represented by Ogilvy & Mather. He sent them a copy and a deal. "If you make the commercial look like an ad for my record, I'll give it to you for free,"[8] Copeland told them. It was up to Jaguar.

Jaguar is also British. Created by William Lyons as a motorcycle side-car company in 1922 with a vision of "creating the closest thing we can to something that is alive."[9] In 1927, they moved to cars (SS1), and in 1935, Jaguar was born. From the C-type of the 1950s, to the E-type of the 1960s, to the XJ and the S-type, Jaguar was a fast and expensive car. "We were starting to move the Jaguar brand into areas where it's never been before—or not for a long time, not since (Jaguar founder) Sir William Lyons handed the keys to an XK129 to Clark Gable" said Roger Putnam, Jaguar's then worldwide director of sales and marketing.[10] While always relatively successful, the Jaguar brand was also aging by 1999 with a desire to move to "a younger, more female oriented customer base"[11] and a fondness for music branding. Jaguar had used everything from Etta James to the Propeller Head. "Etta James is my favorite,"[12] said Al Saltiel, Jaguar's then general marketing manager.

When the pitch came from their agency, Jaguar was already comfortable with music marketing. Etta James "laid the foundation that not only made Jaguar open to use the Sting video, it almost became a necessity because we were already seeing the proof of the effectiveness of music with this brand,"[13] said David Murphy, formerly of Jaguar's advertising agency Ogilvy and Mather. "Jaguar's marketing and advertising people were delighted when they saw [the latest] Sting music video. It showed Sting cruising through the Nevada desert singing his track 'Desert Rose' while sitting in the back seat of a black Jaguar S-type."[14] "The voice-over in the spots and the ad's main line—'What do rock stars dream of'—grew out of the lyrics in Sting's song. 'Desert Rose' is based on a dream," explained Ogilvy & Mather's Anton Crone, describing the ad's theme. "And from that we got the line, 'Everyone dreams of becoming a rock star. What then do rock stars dream of?'" "The answer: riding in a Jaguar S-Type, of course."[15]

Why did Jaguar run with this campaign that literally dropped in their lap?

> For Jaguar in that time, it was really a new category that they had not been into at least for a long time. They were always at the upper end of the market; they were kind of coming into the mid-segment, premium end of the luxury market and staying ... really that effort made the vehicle really well known along with this song.[16]

Why did it make sense or cents?

> I think the first key thing is that, at the end of the day, you need to sell something and this did help sell things and make the brand a lot more emotionally relevant to a younger demographic, so that was another key success. People buying Jags tended to be older. The young people didn't have a problem with it but it was one of those things they would wait for when they were older. The S-type was successful at bringing the medium age of the Jaguar buyer down.[17]

And how did Sting help? As Saltiel said,

> You are always looking for a way to connect consumers emotion-
> ally with your brand and music is a great stimulus. I think that
> connection kind of helps people associate your product category
> and the song helps create the stimulus to do that. In this case,
> it was a song that people knew or didn't know but it was a song
> that they could relate to and more easily associate, remember our
> product.[18]

Copeland agreed

> Jaguar, as other companies had discovered, they could help their
> image by attaching yourself to a song which appeals to the demo
> that you are trying to reach. Obviously, if you have a Rolls Royce,
> you are not going to put a song on there that would appeal to a
> seventeen year old. If you've got a small Fiat that's a $10,000 car
> you are going to try to sell to a lower age demo that doesn't have a
> lot of money. The younger the age then the younger music works
> better. So the art of using music to sell products is really marrying
> the right sort of the impression that the music gives to the impres-
> sion that the product wants to gain, i.e., who are you trying to sell
> your product to, and does the music to appeal to that age group,
> and that demo. If you can marry those two together, then the
> music works for you.[19]

As for Sting, he said that "being in a partnership allowed me to get my
music to more people, it is a beautiful car and it evoked the feeling of style
we were trying to achieve."[20] Jaguar welcomed him with an open car door.
"Sting was delighted to become part of Jaguar's mystique,"[21] said Putnam.
Copeland added that Sting's support came with the fact that "the video
was a Jaguar commercial, but the commercial was a Sting commercial."[22]
Credibility is always a consideration for the artist who never wants to
appear to be "selling out."[23] In this case, it appears that the fit made it
work. Ann Powers wrote in *The New York Times* a that, "Such deals do
not undermine Sting's credibility because they are utterly congruous with

his image. Sting's music is the sound of money well spent."[24] Copeland agreed that

> The major reason it worked was that both the artist and the product fit together very well. Each gained from the other's sort of look. Jaguar gained from the fact that Sting was sort of current, he was much younger then obviously their core base had been. The fact that he was in the Jaguar, that it was a cool hip video. The song hit the charts and the car became hip. It was obviously a major factor in selling the car just as it was selling the music. If you're not hip, you don't sell. So the hip factor worked both from the Sting perspective because the car kind of looked cool and they worked from Jaguar's perspective.[25]

The key factor here was that it started as a video and became a commercial Copeland argues

> The difference between what I did and others have done is that my deal with Jaguar was, "look I'm not going to make a Jaguar commercial, I am going to make a Sting commercial." But here's the point, I've already made a Jaguar commercial because our video is a complete Jaguar commercial. So you don't need to worry about selling your car, I've already done it. So now you focus on selling my artist and we've got a deal. So you'll see in that commercial, that it says from the new Sting album, *Brand New Day*. It's a record commercial, not a car commercial. That was the thing that flipped it. Sting goes "okay it's a TV commercial for my record." It just so happens they're using the video for the car and Jaguar is paying for it. So basically the fact that I had realized (1) that we were dead without something, and (2) that I didn't need to advertise a product because I had already done that inadvertently and if I could get the company to actually advertise the record it was a win/win.[26]

"The deal was a watershed," Copeland says, because while classic hits had long been licensed for commercials, "This was the first time it was an unknown song by a contemporary artist."[27] So instead of $1.8 million to promote the song it was more like $8 million.

> Before making the deal with Jaguar, Sting's record company had planned on selling about 1 million albums. Their marketing and promotion budget had been estimated at about $1.8 million, including $800,000 to make the "Desert Rose" video. Jaguar, by comparison, shelled out about $8 million for the TV commercial time, and gave the song exposure to a global audience Sting might not have reached with its own marketing.[28]

Ogilvy & Mather of New York, Jaguar's advertising agency developed two TV spots—a 30-second and a 60-second version for the "Sting S-Type" campaign.

It first began running on March 20, 2000 in the United States and by August 2000, the ads began appearing internationally. "[The Jaguar] TV commercial proved an excellent piece of marketing, with the song being continually exposed to mainstream TV audiences, who got 30 seconds of prime Sting when they least expected it."[29]

> However, the deal between Sting and Jaguar to run the ads raised some eyebrows, considering that Sting was an avid environmentalist who was endorsing a gas-guzzling vehicle. The Jaguar ads, however, helped turn the tide for "Desert Rose" and the album *Brand New Day*. The ad ran everywhere and people started demanding the song, and it was soon being played on the radio and beyond.[30]

"Desert Rose" lasted over six months "on the U.S. music charts and had 'top ten' showing all across Europe. It became Sting's biggest hit in 10 years. It also lifted the album *Brand New Day* to become one of Sting's best selling ever."[31] By January 2001, the album had sold more than 3 million copies (triple platinum) and to this date it has sold over 4 million copies. The "Desert Rose" single peaked at #15 on the UK singles Chart and #17 on the U.S. Billboard Hot 100. The album *Brand New Day* peaked at #9 on the Billboard 200 and sold over 3.5 million copies in the United States alone. The album also won several Grammys for the year 2000 including Best Pop Vocal Album and Best Male Pop Vocal Performance. At the 2000 Grammy awards ceremony, Sting performed "Desert Rose" with Cheb Mami.

As for the car, in early 2000, at the International Auto Show in New York, Jaguar distributed press kits. It included a "Desert Rose" video and two Jaguar TV ads using the song: a 60-second version and a 30-second version. A promotional CD-single was also included in the packet that had three versions of the song—a radio version at 3:54, an LP version at 4:46, and a club mix version at 4:44 minutes. There were also six 35 mm full color transparencies featuring Sting and car, full color sheets of the same photos, and some Jaguar background information.

> Jaguar for its part, was quite happy to have used the Sting song, and the experience appears to have had an impact on Jaguar's thinking about how to package itself thereafter. Owned by the U.S. auto giant Ford, Jaguar is the venerable U.K. car company known for its luxury cars, but also for its somewhat stuffy image. However, in the last several years, Jaguar has continued to use popular music in other car ads – from Deep Purple's "Hush", a 1968 hit, to Spoon's more current tune, "I Turn My Camera On." Songs by Clash, Queen, Moby and Propellerhead have also been used. Granted, not all of these have worked as well as Sting's "Desert Rose."[32]

But did the collaboration sell cars?

It's hard to say how the campaign lifted sales specifically. But you can note that S-Type doubled sedan sales by offering a model in a new premium price point. Additionally, the typical Jag customer was say 58 years old and with a higher concentration of self-employed compared to our competitors at the time. S-Type coupled with the "Sting campaign" brought in a new demographic closer to 50 ... .[33]

In retrospect people continue to talk about the Sting and Jaguar duet.

Three years is an eternity in the what-have-you-done-for-me-lately environs of Hollywood. But a discussion of entertainment/brand alliances with anyone in the music business is sure to include reverent references to the Sting-Jaguar deal of 2000. It's a touchstone, one that's particularly relevant as music labels aggressively combat the piracy they blame for decimating recorded music sales. There are factors in the decline beyond file-sharing sites and CD burners. Even consumers who legally download songs reject buying a package of 10 songs when what they want is a single. Some blame product quality, saying there's not enough good music. But it's really a marketing issue. It's almost impossible for artists to break through. They can't get radio exposure, and with MTV a lifestyle network, videos are pushed to second-tier channels.[34]

So what's the answer?

There's a broad spectrum of possible solutions with four current favorites. The first is to create quality, legitimate download services (Apple's iTunes is the best so far). Record execs believe people will pay for music if they have choice and convenience. The second is lawsuits against those who pirate music, a step that risks alienating customers. The third is price cuts. Universal Music Group smartly lowered the cost of its CDs by 30%; rivals will almost certainly be forced to follow suit. The fourth path is to align with brands to extend distribution and marketing budgets.[35]

In the case of "Desert Rose," the alignment of band and brand was made and because of it, for good or bad, "Desert Rose" will always be "the song in the Jaguar commercial" as a quick search of concert reviews and blogs attests: "Favorite moment: I remember that *Jaguar commercial.* That was the greatest song *Sting* will ever belt out;"[36] "Desert Rose" (the Jaguar commercial song);"[37] "Younger folks who only know Sting from *Brüno* or that Jaguarcommercial."[38]

1. "At the end of the day, you need to sell something." Miles Copeland
2. "You need to use the music to make the brand more emotionally relevant." Miles Copeland
3. "You are always looking for a way to connect consumers emotionally with your brand, and music is a great stimulus."
4. "The art of using music to sell products is really marrying the right sort of impression that the music gives to the impression that the product wants to gain."

Unknown funny fact: "When I shared what we (Jaguar) wanted to do with the president , he was an older gentleman, didn't know who Sting was, [and I said] you know he's the guy with The Police, and he said well we can't have that!" (Al Saltiel formerly with Jaguar).

Jaguar/Sting Commercial Copy

Sting "Desert Rose" from the album Brand New Day
Everyone dreams of being a rock star
What do rock stars dream of?
Jaguar S-Type

The Art of Performance
www.jaguar.com/us

Jaguar's Ad Music (1999–2008)[39]

"Desert Rose"
Sting
"History Repeating"
Propellerheads & Shirley Bassey

"I Turn My Camera On"
Spoon
"The Girl's Attractive"
Diamond Nights
"Hardcore Days & Softcore Nights"
Aqueduct
"Signs Of Love"
Moby
"I'm In Love With My Car"
Queen
"Battle Without Honor…#2"
Tomoyasu Hotei
"London Calling"
The Clash
"Two Rocks And A Cup Of Water"
Massive Attack
"Hush"
Deep Purple

CHAPTER 9

"Pink Moon" ... Drake and VW (1999)

It is not that unusual for a painter (Vincent van Gogh) or even a writer (Edgar Allan Poe) to become famous after death. It is a bit more rare for a music artist, and even more unique for the fame to be the result of a commercial. Nick Drake was an English singer-songwriter and musician. He recorded three albums: *Five Leaves Left* (1969), *Bryter Layter* (1970), and *Pink Moon* (1972). He died in 1974 at the age of 26. The story might have ended there if it were not for a commercial in 1999.

> In what has to be one of pop music's cruelest ironies, cult folk hero Nick Drake, who overdosed on antidepressants twenty-six years ago after releasing three commercially disappointing albums, is on the verge of scoring his first ever chart hit thanks to a Volkswagen commercial.[1]

And it almost didn't happen, as Alan Pafenbach of the Arnold Agency had originally intended to use *The Church*'s "Under the Milky Way." Maybe it was fate, or just everything in due time as Drake's manager Joe Boyd said. "In a way, maybe the fact that Nick wasn't popular at the time made him not of the time."[2] While Pafenbach and Boyd differ on how it actually was chosen, each has a story.

For 10 years from 1995 to 2005, Alan Pafenbach was the executive creative director at the Arnold Agency in Boston. "I usually get introduced as the 'Volkswagen guy,'"[3] he has said. It is here that the story begins.

> Generally one of the things that advertising agencies do, and they do it more often now than they probably did in the past, is when they are pitching an idea or they are pitching a campaign, where in our case, we are pitching to win the business, you create, what we kind of call ad-like objects—videos that can sort of convey a certain energy and ambiance, something that sort of says this is how we feel the soul of the campaign is going to feel. Music, of course, is really powerful and a kind of short cut right there to your emotional center pretty quickly and efficiently. So, what we do is a lot of times we make these little films that sort of look like these commercials and we did this when we pitched Volkswagen in the first place. Obviously you are on a budget and so what you do is you go to your record collection start to pulling out pieces of music that you think sort of represent the mood and the attitude that you want to convey and that is kind of how we actually won the business originally. So, we didn't invent this but I think we were probably a little earlier to it and it is kind of like a given now. Production was not as desktop as it is now. You still had to go to a production facility. You had to spend some money and you had to spend time and so it sort of was a way to get an edge in a pitch for us to create a video. What you would do is you would take a lot of video material from other people's commercials or movies or anywhere you could kind of find it and then kind of make these collages and you put music to it and so that is how we won the business originally and we did it with a piece of music.

I can't remember the name of the band. We didn't have the music to launch the entire campaign, the driver's live campaign, but that was the methodology to give you a little perspective there. So we became known for using real music in commercials and people did that occasionally but we did it because we thought it was a way to reach the audience. We thought it was more authentic to use real music than to use composed music for advertising. It was a very big distinction at that time between the industry in terms of using composed music and there was an entire industry sort of flying along that side. Then there's the music industry, which produces entertainment, we started to blur the lines. One of the things we used, because we did not have enormous research to buy records from the Talking Heads or something like that, we had to look for obscure music frankly because it was something that would sound fresh to people, it would be something that they hadn't heard a thousand times and that they hadn't formed associations but we would still have the composed artistic and emotional reasons not personal reasons. So Nick Drake was one of those artists. He was sort of a singer/songwriter's singer/songwriter but he wasn't very well known. He had passed away back in the 70's after a small body of work. People who knew music knew him but he wasn't as widely known, wasn't a Top 40 phenomenon by any means. So that was kind of the impress we took with a lot of things. We just kind of find this authentic music usually sort of underground or under-appreciated and elevated it and put it with images and created a commercial that was more of an ambiance then it was about selling specific issues.[4]

Who did come up with Nike Drake?

It has been so long and so many people were involved in the creation of that commercial between the creative team and nobody really can specifically say who found that piece of music. I do know that it was my partner Lance and Shane Hutton, who was the copywriter at the time. I think they both sort of came up with it. We tried a couple of things. Another person who has a lot of influence in these kinds of things is the actual video editor. We used to use a fellow named Andre Betz in New York. And sometimes he would bring music because he would start cutting something and he would need something to put it to and so he would just go into his collection and start to pull things out. In this case, this was something we gave to him but in the past he has been known to give it to other editors who are actually pretty good and understand music and obviously because they work in a medium where for pacing and rhythm and tempo is important. They have a secret stash in the back of their heads, with some pieces of music that will fit different kinds of moods and tempos for cut. In that case, Andre had to take this piece of music and basically kind of cut it up. None of these things just come off the record because usually songs are written with a structure, an introduction and a middle, and bridge and whatever. Often the editor has to figure how to take the music apart and put it back together so that it fit the thirty seconds or sixty seconds, or something like that but not destroy the song. So that was part of his contribution. I am sure that a purist who really knows the song would probably say those lyrics came before those lyrics and the bridge is in the wrong place but in the end you sort of preserve the intent. So that was his role and so everybody kind of works together and obviously the pictures are important, which is where I came in, in terms of creating a look and feel and a mood, just from a video standpoint. Our commercial was directed by Jonathan Dayton and Valerie Faris who went on to win an Academy award for *Little Miss Sunshine*. They still keep their feet firmly planted in the commercial world but they started out in music videos. They were used to creating imagery sort of visual tableaus. I think there was a national cinematographers was a fellow named Lance Acord who is now a director on his own and is actually doing movies now. There are a bunch of people who were really good at making music and images work together on that particular commercial. The assignment originally was a regional retail commercial to clear out the last convertibles, Cabrio Convertibles, because the Beetle was a convertible and that was coming and there was another convertible coming, and that was going to be Volkswagen's convertible. So it had like a sales point which would sort of promote this, promote convertibles, and get people to buy them and when we were done with it, it was such a piece. There was so must emotion and sort of transcended convertibles are great that it became kind of that it became kind of a significant piece anyway in terms of representing the brand attitudes and values, that kind of thing and so it became much bigger than it originally started out as an assignment being, which is often the case. It is kind of the lightning in a bottle kind of a thing. You sort of work on it and then it just sort of becomes and you just sort of go with it. When we saw initial footage and when we started putting music to it ... I will back up a little bit because our intention originally was to put one of the songs that was in the mix was done by *The Church*, but it was a little gloomy. So it is funny the commercial sort of gets interchangeably, they called it "Pink Moon" or "Milky Way," depending on who you talk to and originally "Milky Way," I think, was sort of had the lead. But when we got into the edits with Andre, he kind of said, well, I tried it with this and I tried it with that and I think this one works better and we watched it and it is just sort of there, it sort of becomes obvious, when it gets put together, things just sort of ... the moments in the song line up with moments in the visuals and the mood just sort of comes across and it is always amazing to see what happens when you put the music and the picture together. Whenever I watch a movie now, I always find myself somewhere in the movie imagining the movie without that music or the moment without that music and you can sort of see ... you can't ... at some point the two just sort of merge and some movies would be very different movies. I was just watching "House of Cards" the other night and David Fincher just sort of makes very interesting music choices on the movies that he is affiliated with whether it was the "Social Network" or anything. You can't really imagine how that would work with any other kind of music. At first some songs don't age well because the music choice was so specific to an era that you have a hard time kind of ... it kind of sticks out and other movies, the music is timeless. I think the fact that Nick Drake was already that song that was written in 1972 and this was 1999 and so the song was almost 20 years old at the time. An acoustic guitar and a single voice just never will go out of style. So it just works. One of the things was that it was a generational. It crossed generations because it wasn't Nirvana "Team Spirit." People, baby boomers and parents of baby boomers can sort of relate to it. In that way some of these very simple classic types of pieces of music with acoustic instruments can really transcend time and make these things still work years later.[5]

Is this the way music gets selected?

As we were going through production, even probably on set, we would be sitting over in the corner listening. Lance would have a bunch of music and we would sit there and listen to it and that's kind of interesting. You really don't know, you don't even know what the film is going to look like. Honestly, that shoot was something where we didn't even know what we were going to have. It had a story line. It was sort of born from this recollection that Lance had about riding around in a convertible at night and he said that was the great thing about convertibles is the top down on the way to the beach, that's one thing but one of the really cool things about convertibles is when you drive around at night. I felt that was going to be a great vibe and we had sort of scenes, wouldn't it be cool if this happened or that happened, but I said it needs a beginning and an end in some way, it needs a story line to it. So that's where you sort of come upon these people and you see these four people and what is interesting how we cast. You're doing a casting and you put four card table chairs down and we have four actors and randomly you go, you, you and you sit down and you look at each person and that person might work for the driver, and that person might work. In this case we brought these four kids in and sat them down in the position as if they were and what we liked about it was it didn't really seem to make sense that any of them would actually be friends because they were all very different. There was kind of the all-American blond cheerleader kind of girl, and then there was this sort of like kind of funky, dark, artsy looking guy driving, and then sort of like a nice look-ing kid in the backseat looks kind of naïve and there was this kind of very very cool and controlled African American girl in the front seat and it just was just like what scenario would these people ever be together and we kind of came to the conclusion that they all met over the summer and were working at a restau-rant or something. They had been thrown together out of college and they weren't friends at the beginning of the summer but this was the end of the summer and that they were basically going to go and split up and probably never see each other again and this was sort of this one last night they were going to all go to a party and you could imagine that this kind of thing could happen in Nantucket. So that is why it has this sort of the ocean and water. In fact the house that we found, we shot north of San Francisco on the Sebago Bay. So we tried to make it look kind of island. You go back and look at the commercial and you look at the house, the house is sort of this shingle style Cape Cod house, probably has some lobster crap on the porch or something like that. This is all details probably lost on most people. It was a part for us because we wanted to make it authentic. We wanted to give the actors a sense of who they were and what they were doing. We put this sort of naive kid in the backseat with the beautiful blond girl and you could tell he had kind of a crush on her all summer long. The driver is in a band and he's cool. I mean it is just interesting you sort of make up stories about who all of the people are, and then somehow the music just glues it all together.[6]

Did Nick Drake sell out?

So one of the wonderful consequences of that was that Nick Drake's music became visible probably more than when he was alive and we had to negotiate with his estate for the music. His sister was actually the person who controlled the rights to the music and so she had to actually approve it. When you use real music from real bands, especially at that time, there was still a lot of sensitivity about "selling out" or anything like that and we got turned down a lot. Until people started to figure out that, especially the record companies started to figure out that this was a way … they were starting to get challenged by digital music and Napster and stuff like that and their sales are going down and the market is changing and they started to figure out that this was a great way to boost their catalog and so they had music that was in there already and if we didn't buy it, then it would just sit there making no money. Oasis turned us down. We literally offered them a million dollars and they would not take it and actually one of them would take it but since they don't get alone as soon as one said yes and the other one said no. People started to see the kind of commercials we were making, and how we were using the music, and how the music was respected especially since a lot of these musicians were not getting a lot of air play on traditional radio and stuff like that, they were like, hey this is a way for my music that doesn't get out there much to get out there and so it started to be that people would start to seek us out. Then we have record producers calling us up and saying hey we have this funky little group and they are doing this and how about using them and stuff like that and so it started to change the way the music industry started to think about it and it definitely improved awareness for Nick Drake.[7]

Did you pay a millions dollars for "Pink Moon?"

It was not a million dollars. We would be doing deals for tens of thousands of dollars, not hundreds of thousands of dollars. Occasionally we paid five figures, but we never paid seven. Actually, no, a lot of money would be a $100,000 or $200,000. Remember a TV commercial itself would only cost maybe $300,000. The percentage of the music couldn't be too much, but that was where it was great to be using more obscure music because from the point of view, the person who always held the music was like it is not making me anything right now so if I can get $50,000 for this, and it boosts record sales then it's win-win. If it doesn't diminish the reputation of the artist and it enhances the song, why not?

Nowadays, the intersection of commercial music and entertainment music is sort of assumed. Movies are built around sound tracks that are going to be released. I mean we probably released probably one of the first commercial sound tracks. We actually put out a VW CD with like ten or twelve tracks that we had used on commercials. Up until that time, people just didn't think about it that way. Musicians didn't think about it that way. There's a lot of people doing kind of that sort of ambient story telling kind of stuff. It sort of almost gone its course a bit. There's a million kind of folky, frail girl singer songs out there. You can find them and throw them on a vitamin commercial, and you could throw them on whatever. It is sort a format now, but at that time that wasn't the kind of music that got used in commercials. The most famous thing that I could think of was when Nissan did that animated, stop animation commercial, for the Z which I think at the time they weren't even making. They were using David Lee Rush. That is sort of unusual, because usually the music was bigger than the brand, the music was the big brand, to pay for, to get a piece of music from a music company was expensive. Especially something that everybody knew it was a hit. Now, since the music industry and the radio industry is kind of atomized into millions and millions of formats I suppose if you wanted to buy a Justin Timberlake song. If you think about it, there isn't a lot of top music that makes it into commercials, even the biggest brands. Pepsi can get the Beyonce, but that is about it. The auto industry doesn't spend money that way.[8]

Joe Boyd was Drake's producer (as well as Muddy Waters's, Bob Dylan's, Eric Clapton's, Pink Floyd's, REM's and others producer). He has a slightly different memory of how "Milky Way" became "Pink Moon."

First of all, let me set the scene. Originally I produced the records. I did not produce "Pink Moon." That was done after I left for California and Nick just went in with the engineer and just made his record in two days, just acoustic playing the guitar and singing. I had moved to California. So I wasn't directly involved with

making that record. In subsequent years, when I came back I
started my own label called Hannibal in 1980. I sold my production company, Witchseason Productions which produced Nick's
records. Nick's "Pick Moon" is produced under Witchseason,
which is how the song was connected to me. I sold it to Island
Records and one of the conditions of the sales was that they would
never delete Nick's records. The records had not sold. They had
been a flop, but I believed that one day, what did happen, would
happen. So when I started my label, I started it as a sort of under
the umbrella of Island in 1980 so that I was back in touch with
Island while working with Island. I pointed out to them that they
didn't have Nick's records available in America. So they agreed,
therefore, to let me license Nick's records for America, for North
America, and release them on the Hannibal label. I also got them
to let me put out the box set which had been released in 1978
but then they ran out of cardboard parts and they deleted it. I
re-released the box set of Hannibal in the UK and distributed
it throughout Europe. Island still had the original three albums
available through Island UK. So Nick's catalog was partly available
through me, exclusively available through Hannibal, in North
America and to a lesser extent in the UK. During the course of
the next ten years I worked more and more closely as the interest
grew and the kind of market for Nick's music grew. I developed a
good working relationship with Gabrielle Drake, who was Nick's
sister, who was the executrix of the estate. People began coming
out of the woodwork and saying, let's make a movie about Nick's
story. Gabrielle and I would talk about it and we kind of agreed
there wasn't really a movie to be made there. But we would con-
sult about offers and proposals and licensing and things that came
up, Gabrielle and I would talk. Then in 1991, Hannibal Records
sold it, merged it with, and basically was swallowed by Ryko Disk
which was a leading independent American company. As part of
that deal, it was kind of a complicated deal, but the end result was
that I got the publishing rights to Nick's songs back from Island
who owned them. And those rights were then sold to Ryko Disc
as part of Ryko Disc's taking over Hannibal. So by the mid-90s,

I was a Director of Ryko Disc, Hannibal, the label, was part of Ryko Disc. We still have the catalog exclusively in America and some of, part of, the catalog in the UK. We also controlled the publishing. There's two rights you need. You need the publishing rights and you need the master rights—the right to the performance of the song, the right to the composition of the song. So by this time, Nick's records are selling more and more and more. It wasn't huge but it was still we were selling like 30–40 thousand year to year, that kind of thing, across the whole catalog, across all territories. There were a few films (see list). We had a few sync licenses, people who made films. And as a footnote, let me say that I was a big fan of Neil Young's *This Note's for You*, which expressed contempt for artists who allow their selves to be used for corporate purposes. So at some point in 1997, I got a call from somebody in the Business Affairs Department of Ryko Disc, saying that Volkswagen, their ad agency, wanted to use "Pink Moon" in a Volkswagen ad. I really didn't think very long about it, I just thought forget about it. Nick's music in a car ad, you must be joking. They said okay. Then like a few days later, I got another call from the Business Affairs Department, the ad agency was unwilling to take no for an answer. They asked if it would be okay if they sent me a storyboard. Before I just turned it down without knowing what it was, just on general principles, would I look at the story board? And I said, "Well, sure why not." There was no harm in that. I received a courier package in England with this story board of the ad, pretty much the way the ad flows, the way they edited it out. I looked at it and I can't remember what there was in the cover letter, whether I needed an explanation to walk me through it or whether it was obvious from the storyboard itself. When I kind of stopped finished looking at it, I called the Business Affairs Department at Ryko Disc and I said, "Will you ask them if I am understanding this correctly? My impression from reading the storyboard is that the only sound in the ad from beginning to end will be Nick's music, that there is no voice over, there is no other voice, but Nick's from beginning to end, not even after the music finishes. This seems a little wild to me, can you confirm that I am reading this thing correctly?" They said yes, okay, and so they got back to me the next day and they said, yes, we spoke to the people in the ad agency. So they confirmed that my impression was correct, that there would be no other sound or voice in the ad other than Nick's voice. So I thought that is kind of an interesting thing, let me talk to Gabrielle. So I called Gabrielle and I described the storyboard to her and I described the whole thing and I told her about my initial sort of major response, as to reject the idea out of hand but that looking at this story board and understanding what they wanted to do, I sort of thought well why not. We want Nick's music to get out there as widely as possible and this seems to be remarkably tasteful as an ad. If you are ever going to do an ad, this is unusually appropriate, or at least acceptable way, that it can be done. So we gave the thumbs up. First we negotiated the rights, whatever the fee was, I can't remember what it was. I think it was like a step deal, where they pay a certain amount for using it for a trial period and then if they renewed it and they used it more, they pay a bunch more money, whatever it was. So that all was done and the next thing you know the thing was in use. My recollection is that it was used only on cable TV, never network and it was never used in Britain. I am not sure if it was used in other countries besides the US but my understanding was that it was used on cable television in the US.[9]

And did the commercial sell the song?

We noticed an obvious uptick in Nick's sales in the coming year and a lot of comment came in, a lot of dialog, a lot of feedback, all very positive, and a huge surge in sales. I think the year before the ad we sold, 25,000 units or whatever, and the year of the ad, we sold like 85,000 units of Nick's music. Still to this day, you get people who say the first time I heard Nick's music was in that Volkswagen ad. That is when a lot of people first heard it. Anyway, so then what happened was that about a year later, maybe more a year and a half later, by this time Ryko Disc have gotten and I am not totally sure of the chronology of the years here. My memory is about '98 or maybe it was '97, I am not sure. Anyway, a year and a half after that, Ryko by this time had rashly taken on Capital Investors, bank loans. Bought the Frank Zappa catalog and was in this sort of death spiral of kind of venture capital, bank loans, big graphs on the walls, had projections, going upward like a Swiss Alp. Then, of course, they would never be met and the record company would have to be sold in the end. But this time there was a kind of combination of optimism and desperation to ramp up the sales in the general size and output of the company. It turned out the ad agency that had done the "Pink Moon" was based in Boston and Ryko's headquarters, the main office was in Salem, Massachusetts, just up the road. I was on my way to Salem for a conference and I got a message during my visit with a team of people, a group of people from Ryko Disc, the managing director, me and the head of marketing, and somebody else were going to make a visit to the ad agency because we were in discussions with them about them taking on building up Ryko's image and sort of brainstorming ways that they could help build the Ryko brand. It was one of those things that I don't think anything ever came of it but it was an idea for a meeting. So they all drove in one morning to Boston and went to this kind of movie, warehouse type of space down by the water front in Boston and we went into this meeting room and people came in with coffee, etc. I was introduced to these people who were all kind of young. I remember one person that I was introduced to and I don't remember his name, he was wearing a lumberjack shirt and a kind of bobble hat, those rural hats, and he was introduced to me as the guy who had had the idea for "Pink Moon" and Volkswagen. So before the formal meeting began, we are all sitting around just shooting the breeze and I said, "Tell me how did you ... how did this all come down?" The story that he told me was that the storyboard and the whole cost of the ad had been constructed around a record by a group called *The Church*, who are an Australian group and I remembered the name of the record as "Midnight Ride," but someone when I told the story corrected me and said they have a track called not the "Night Ride," called "Night Ride" or something.

I can't remember the name of the song. There is a song that was
sort of more literally about what you see in the ad and that they
had spent quite a bit of time and energy constructing this ad
around this track by this group. My memory of what this guy
told me, it was the night before the presentation to Volkswagen
that the Volkswagen account executive was on his way from New
York coming up to Boston the next day. This guy could be part
of the team that had created this ad was sitting at home smoking
a joint and he put on "Pink Moon," the LP, and he was playing
it through and he got to the track "Pink Moon" and he had this
eureka moment. He thought this would work even better than
that track by *The Church*. The next morning he came in early with
the Pink Moon record, got the creative team assembled, played
them the record and said, "I think we should go with this track
instead of *The Church* track," and this was the morning of the presentation. Everybody kind of went yea, cool, let's do it. So when
the Volkswagen executives come for the presentation, they didn't
have to do anything, they stuck with the same story board but
they swapped in the Nick Drake track and Volkswagen went for it
and the rest, you know the story.[10]

So if Nick was alive when that call came in, do you think he would
have agreed to do it?

Sure, I think so. Nick wanted to succeed. The image of him as
a kind of delicate artist who was above the fray. The fact that he
was very shy and wasn't a good performer that didn't mean that
he didn't want to sell lots of records. He definitely did. He would
have seen exactly that he wouldn't have to perform live. He could
get out to a lot of people. I don't think he would have had any
worries about it.[11]

And would you do it again today?

So many varieties that we tell about the music industry twenty
years ago don't really apply anymore. It is like I used to think

you shouldn't release an out-takes and demos from an artist unless they are really, really good. And now there's no point in having an opinion on that because everything is out there and circulating without any curation or control and so those sort of ideas are kind of pointless. If I was managing an artist today, being in an ad is one of the few ways you really can get across to a lot of people at once in such fragmented market place, how else are you going to do it? I think Neil Young's even done it. I kind of shutter at the idea of that is what you got to do, it is just the truth of the matter, that that's what people do these days and without really blinking and I probably would too if I was trying to build an artist at the moment. But one of the many reasons why I still live in Britain, one of the reasons is the BBC. The ability to actually turn the television on and not see any commercials.[12]

However it happened, it was an excellent commercial:

Fade in to a moonlit river, an isolated bridge, and a carload of recent college graduates. Acoustic guitar strums, both urgent and plaintive, are joined by a husky voice, uttering lyrics that border on making rational sense but never quite get there: "Saw it written and saw it say, pink moon is on its way." When the voice intones "pink moon," the camera points skyward and we see from the perspective of the passengers a bright full moon, the light of which fills the clear night sky. The music and visuals evoke a feeling of quiet magic and mystery, enhanced by the hazy purpose of what we're seeing. The four young people pull up to their destination—a party that seems excessively boisterous by comparison to the enchanting ride that brought them there. They hesitate, glance at each other, and silently communicate their shared wish for more backroads, more moonlight, more windblown hair, and, presumably, more of the beautiful music that has continued to play throughout this quietly dramatic scene. They drive off to embrace what they have decided is more valuable in this moment. They choose the journey over the destination. At this point, it's still unclear what exactly we're seeing. Finally, nearly a full minute into the piece, the famous Volkswagen logo appears against the same starry sky the moon has been filling. Volkswagen. The Cabrio. Drivers Wanted. We instantly recall that the car has been the focal point of their shared communing with the night.[13]

1. "Music is really powerful and a kind of short cut right there to your emotional center pretty quickly and efficiently." Alan Pafenbach
2. "Some songs don't age well because the music choice is so specific to an era; An acoustic guitar and a single voice just never will go out of style." Alan Pafenbach
3. "It doesn't diminish the reputation of the artist … it enhances the song. Now a days it is the intersection of commercial music and entertainment music." Alan Pafenbach
4. "I was a big fan Neil Young's 'This Notes for You,' which expressed contempt for artists who allow their selves to be used for corporate purposes." Joe Boyd

Nick Drake's Songs in Films

Lake House (2006) "Pink Moon" and "Time Has Told Me"
Fever Pitch (2005) "Northern Sky"
Garden State (2004) "One of These Things First"
My Name is Tanino (2002) "Cello Song"
Oesters van Nam Kee (2002) "River Man"
True Dreams (2002) "Cello Song"
The Good Girl (2002) "Black Eyed Dog"
Me Without You (2001) "Cello Song"
The Royal Tenenbaums (2001) "Fly"
Serendipity (2001) "One of These Things First" and "Northern Sky"
Crush (2001) "One of These Things First"

Ratcatcher (1999) "Cello Song"
Practical Magic (1998) "Black Eyed Dog"
Hideous Kinky (1998) "Road"
Le Ciel est a Nous (1997) "Saturday Sun"
Dream With the Fishes (1997) "River Man"

Kicking & Screaming (1995) "Time of No Reply"
http://www.nickdrake.com/talk/viewtopic.php?t=3608&start=0

CHAPTER 10

"Find My Baby" ... Moby and American Express (2000)

"When *Play* was released, I kind of thought my career was over," says Moby.

The week *Play* was released, it sold, worldwide around 6,000 copies. Eleven months after *Play* was released, it was selling 150,000 copies a week. I was on tour constantly, drunk pretty much the entire time and it was just a blur. And then all of a sudden movie stars started coming to my concerts and I started getting invited to fancy parties and suddenly the journalists who wouldn't return my publicist's calls were talking about doing cover stories. It was a really odd phenomenon.[1]

Play has since gone platinum in 26 countries, and its success proves two things. First, Moby is an astute businessman willing to make commercial concessions to get his music heard. Second, the average listener has an appetite for vastly different styles of music—from Britney's bubble gum to OutKast's rap and funk to Moby's edgy rock and techno—if only someone would serve them. "It's a classic commercial approach," says Moby. "You look at a cultural scenario and see a strange void."[2]

One of the songs on *Play* is "Find My Baby" of which Moby said:

Basically just me playing slide guitar over a vocal sample. I added what I thought were hip-hop drums to it. In the '80s I was DJing a lot of hip-hip. At one point I was working at Mars and I used to keep a microphone by the turntables. Big Daddy Kane and Run-D.M.C. and 3rd Bass and Flavor Flav and everybody would go to this club and get drunk, and I had the microphone. I was the weird white DJ for all these rappers where were drinking and rapping to impress their girlfriends.[3]

But was it the music or the marketing? "I thought *Play* might sell 200,000 copies worldwide," Moby says. "There was no strategy involved. They called us up and said, 'Can we use your song in this commercial?'" Marci Weber and Barry Taylor, Moby's managers, disagree.

Even before the release of *Play*, with its record-setting run of commercially licensed songs, Weber says the strategy was core to the organization. In 1996, for instance, they received reports that Moby's atmospheric "God Moving Over the Face of the Waters," which sustained the climactic scene in Michael Mann's *Heat*, had made an enormous impression on the film-music community. So during that year's Slamdance film festival, Weber and Taylor "invited every music supervisor in Hollywood" to a party to increase their client's visibility. "We put on this free show, big dinner, all that." When it came to selling Moby's music to soundtracks, Weber adds, the event "was a breaking point." With *Play*, three years later, the managers took the formula and turned the album into an industry. They had seen Moby's first three major-label albums ignored by radio and *Play* rejected by record company after record company. So, says Taylor, "we made a conscious effort to create a marketing plan that had nothing to do with radio." "Porcelain" tinkled away for Bailey's Irish Cream and Nordstrom; "Find My Baby" was hooking hipster consumers for American Express.[4]

In 2001, American Express announced in a press release of the ad that would eventually win a Clio award that year:

American Express and Tiger Woods pair up in a new television advertisement that will launch on the NBA Finals on June 7. The commercial shows Woods playing the toughest course in the world—the streets of Manhattan. The ad, shot on location in New York in late April, shows Woods wallop a golf ball from Park Avenue to Central Park to Wall Street and finally to the Brooklyn Bridge where he putts it into a traditional diner-style blue coffee cup as if he played this fictional Manhattan "golf course" on a regular basis. "Tiger is admired for his ability to do extraordinary things, on the golf course and off. He inspires all of us to create our own success," said John Hayes, executive vice president of Global Advertising for American Express. "The ad reinforces the aspirations of our Cardmembers who dream big, take on challenges and get the job done no matter how big the task." The 60-second television commercial will launch Wednesday, June 7 during the NBA finals. Like the previous ads that are part of the "Moments of Truth" campaign, this Woods ad was directed by Joe Pytka and created by Ogilvy & Mather. American Express' relationship with Woods began in May 1997 when he was signed as a global spokesperson for the company. His first commercials were for American Express Financial Advisors, one of which included his father. His work with American Express includes print advertising and appearances for American Express at the World Golf Championship events.[5]

In 2000, Richard Leiby in the Washington Post described the song and the commercial this way:

The voice in the commercial is a pure blues wail, carrying all the pain of a hard, black life in the Delta. The words are plaintive and muddied: "I'm gonna find my baby—woooo!—before the sun goes down." The face on the TV screen connotes pure success: It's Tiger Woods, golf genius and multimillionaire spokesman for American Express. He's duffing around Manhattan, smiling as he sinks a putt into a throwaway cup on the Brooklyn Bridge, while the bluesman wails.[6]

And what does Moby sample?

The song in question is "Joe Lee's Rock," and it is part of a treasure trove of recordings made in the Deep South by the legendary folk music collector Alan Lomax. It was exhumed and sampled by a vegan techno musician named Moby—who titled his version "Find My Baby." The song helped push Moby's latest album to triple-platinum status (more than three million copies sold worldwide).[7]

And what was the response? "It's been very successful," says Desiree Fish, spokesperson for American Express. "We're getting a million calls from people asking, 'What is that music?' They told people it's Moby."[8]

Note

How does Moby feel about the marketing of *Play* now?

There's a little bit of confusion around the licensing. I'll do interviews and almost everyone says, "So, you licensed every song off of *Play* for commercials," I licensed some of the music to commercials, and to be honest with you, I regret having done that. Just because it's become an odd cross to bear. Mick Jagger in 1965 got endorsed by Coke and got on stage and drank Coca-Cola. People have been selling out for a long time. The irony is that now I don't license my songs to commercials and everybody else does. Once bitten, twice shy. I should have taken lessons from the cool indie-rockers who only license their music to countries where they don't speak English. The hip artists revered by your contemporaries? They license their music, they just do it in South Korea.[9]

Dispelling the belief that his team simply rubber-stamped any and all requests to use songs from *Play*, Moby adds, "We said no to quite a lot of things. There was a Swedish commercial for Bernaise sauce and they wanted to use one of the songs. I was like, 'Oh no, I can't even stoop that low.'"[10]

1. "Dream big, take on challenges and get the job done no matter how big the task." *John Hayes*
2. "I regret having done that." Moby
3. No comment. Tiger Woods

CHAPTER 11

"Days Go By" ... Dirty Vegas and Mitsubishi (2002)

Courtesy of the Richard Phillips Studios.

Dirty Vegas was a British group. Mitsubishi was a Japanese car. How a Californian advertising agency brought them together could only happen in the pictures of motion ... .

It was the fall of 2001, and the Deutsch agency needed a song. Eric Hirshberg, former co-CEO and Creative Officer takes it from there:

> Things needed to happen and we thought what is really leading to a trend that we were seeing, a cultural thing that was at the time was kind of trans-hip hop, dance music. You are with three people who are passing the dance from the back seat to the passenger seat to the driver's seat to this song and then we went on a big music search to find the perfect songs for pop and rock and we found the Dirty Vegas song. So we thought this is the perfect music. It was hypnotic and dreamlike. I think, when we first envisioned it, we envisioned it being a little more hip hop and a little bit higher octane, if you will. But that really took it in a very moody direction

which then with the night time shooting and the streaking lights, we really kind of lead into that dreamlike state. It was sort of singing in car, to dancing in cars, to cars as destination and the whole thing was designed to be a very attractive magnetic environment that you wanted to be a part of, but the fact that you haven't heard the music was really integral to the idea. It wouldn't have worked half as well if it was a song that you knew the words to because it made the people and the brand more intriguing. They were exposing you to new things: new music, new band, new dance moves. It just felt like that's what fashion forward people do in their lives. Someone has those friends that always seemed to have the new band that you want to know about, are always telling you to see the new movie they are recommending that you hadn't heard of. We wanted Mitsubishi to become that brand.[1]

And thanks to that agency for finding that song, Mitsubishi did become that brand. But how that band became that band, and that song became that song is where this story really begins. Dirty Vegas formed in 2001 made up of Ben Harris and Paul Harris (no relation) on instruments and production and Steve Smith on vocals. Steve Smith described how in 2002 to VH1:

I was a percussionist playing in clubs and working with Ben, who's a studio wizard. I've known Paul as a DJ on the UK club scene for years. I was booked to do this gig in Switzerland, and when I got to the airport I saw Paul sitting there in the lounge with his record boxes. It turned out we were both going to the same gig. We had a real good time, so we started working on tracks when we got back to London. "Days Gone By" was one of the first ones out of the bag, and the band was born! We were actually called Dirty Harry, but Warner Bros. or somebody said we couldn't use the name. So we were in this casino in London's West End, knocking drinks back, and we're like, "We've got to find a name for the band!" Paul came running back from the roulette table with lots of English pounds in his hand and said, "It's like Vegas around here!" We loved that seedy side of gambling and the name fit.[2]

When Dirty Vegas released *Days Gone By* in 2001 it was, as Steve Smith describes, "a lukewarm release."[3] At the same time, Deutsch was looking for a song, in a hotel room watching videos, and according to Smith:

That winter of 2001, a guy from Deutsch was in the Netherlands as far we were told at the time at the Light One Nine Hotel. He sees the MTV videos and sees our video and thought Wow, that's something that is worth repeating to maybe more of the campaigns and that just happened to be Mitsubishi one. So the video got played to Mitsubishi. They loved the song and that whole kind of thing and we got the call around Christmas of 2001. We are like "a car commercial in the US?" We weren't really sure at the time because it seemed funny. You are going back ten or eleven years. There were so many stigmas attached to making music to be used for commercials. It was a very, very un-cool thing to do at the time and may not be the number one platform to launch. We were skeptical to say the least. What happened next was they sent us over some of the previous campaigns for Mitsubishi and we saw what they were doing. It was kind of a fresh approach at the time to the car and it was more of a life style campaign. So we saw that it was a way to span a wide cliental. To be honest, we just loved the whole imagery and how it is being shot and we liked where this could be going for us. I loved to see our soul married to Mitsubishi imagery and, with hindsight now, it was a huge success.

I mean the song, it just caught fire, and at the time, there was no electronic music on American radio. There wasn't. There wasn't a spot for it. There was no market place. So there was no way for us to get our music out there and here we are, having that song being used on a $26 million campaign for a new car![4]

The new car was the Eclipse. But Mitsubishi was far from a new company. The Mitsubishi company was first established as a shipping firm by Yatarō Iwasaki in 1870. In 1873, its name was changed to *Mitsubishi*. The name Mitsubishi consists of two parts: *mitsu* meaning *three* and *hishi* meaning *water caltrop*. It is also translated as *three diamonds*. Mitsubishi Motors Corporation is a multinational automaker headquartered in Minato, Tokyo, Japan. The Mitsubishi Eclipse was a sport compact car that was in production between 1989 and 2011. A convertible body style was added for the 1996 model year. It was named after an unbeaten 18th-century English racehorse which won 26 races.

Maybe it's karma that a car named after an English racehorse should have a British band in its commercial. It may have been a predetermined marriage that began when Deutsch got the Mitsubishi account. Current Deutsch CEO Mike Sheldon tells how it all began:

We got the Mitsubishi car account in about 1998. If you looked at those vehicles relative to Toyotas and Hondas and Mazdas and Nissans, we knew that, from a quality perspective, we were never going to be able out-quality the Honda, or out-quality Toyota. But if you look at those cars, they were just a little bit cooler, the sheet metal was bent just a little bit more interestingly. The car was designed to have a little bit more personality and a little bit more flare. If you didn't know, if you were a Martian that came down from outer space and you looked at all the Hondas and Toyotas and Mitsubishis, you would swear the Mitsubishi should be a higher selling car just because it is better looking. So our strategy for them became very simple. Cool cars for cool people. We said we are not going to be able to be a Honda or Toyota beater but we can be an alternative. We could be an alternative that appeals to people who just live life in a slightly more vital way, slightly more vital people. So the idea was to not center so much on features and benefits but more on just the fact that when you buy these cars, they are just a little bit better looking and then they feel cool. So that began a very deliberate music-driven campaign idea where music became as important as any other feature in advertising. So the car was there with great looking aspirational looking people, and really killer music.[5]

Hirshberg continues:

What we did was we said, okay Mitsubishi, I think at the time had a 1% market share, and with a 1% market share, you probably weren't going to be able to out Toyota Toyota or out Honda Honda. What they could do is present a sort of pop cultural alternative to those things. Those things are seen as very mainstream; they are seen as your mom and dad's car. And where Mitsubishi had seen going forward was this kind of very aggressive adolescent board race or styling. And so we thought okay, let's lead into that. Instead of trying to say whatever other challenger brand was doing at the time, saying it has more rear seat leg room than a Toyota Camry or something like that, we said, no, what these things are is they are cooler, they are more expressive and there are fewer of them on the road which means you are going to stand out and make a fashion statement essentially by driving one. So really we are making, I think, the world's first fashion ad for cars and the first campaign that really acknowledged that cars are a big expensive fashion statement and yet there are all kinds of utilities and safety and performance that also goes into our decision. You know what you do is you drive the one that feels right; you drive the one that you want to wear every day. And so we thought could we take youth culture and alternative youth culture and position it to be as an alternative youth brand. That is what led us to the strategy of utilizing essentially unknown music in our commercials.[6]

And then Mitsubishi CEO Pierre Gagnon loved the song.

I still play it on my iPod. I mean it brings back great memories and that was a record year. That was the best year Mitsubishi ever had and we were on a roll, things were going really well. So you have to give credit to most of the outside help. When I went back with Mitsubishi in 1997 we were on the rocks. Our first approach was let's define the brand, who are we, let's work on our strengths. So I had taken on Deutsch at that point, and I said to Deutsch what our grand statement was going to be. We went up tremendously during that period of time and so there were a lot of measurements that would solidify the point that the advertising was working. You know advertising doesn't always work. Deutsch did just a masterful job and the genius behind all that was Erik Hirshberg.[7]

Mitsubishi debuted the 30-second spot with the now famous female "popping" in the passenger seat of the Eclipse March 11, 2002 on national television. Dirty Vegas delayed their self-titled album release three months in the United States to wait for the commercial's release. The results speak for themselves.

With its ad agency, Deutsch Inc., Mitsubishi Motors connected with its target audience by pairing fun, upbeat music with its ad campaigns. In the face of stiff competition from Mitsubishi's rivals, these ads were the catalyst for an upswing for Mitsubishi Motors. In three years, brand awareness grew from 44 percent to 60 percent, and sales increased 70 percent.[8]

Sheldon cheers, "Sales just skyrocketed."[9] Hirshberg agrees, "I think they doubled their market shares."[10] Gagnon confirms:

It was very successful and it ran through a period of five consecutive years of record sales, peaking in 2002 with 45,000 vehicles when all of these campaigns sort of peaked. We had positioned the market properly and then we used our advertising to support the program.[11]

The song "Days Go By" became a radio hit in 2002, peaking at #14 in the United States and #16 in the United Kingdom, and received the Grammy Award for Best Dance Recording. Steve Smith gives all credit to the ad.

We had gone from the song coming out and pretty much not doing anything to appear on Jay Leno to Dave Letterman to Carson Daly to Regis and Kelly and being nominated for MTV awards and winning the Grammy. We would not have had any of that.[12]

And let's not forget the now infamous parody on the Dave Chappelle Show. The song in the Mitsubishi ad had been "woven into the popular culture"[13] as Hirshberg told Advertising Age in 2002.

But why did it work?

First, it wasn't the only time Mitsubishi used popular music in its advertising. Gagnon first hired Deutsch, they brought the music.

Our first launch with them was 1989 and it was all music. It was more than just the music, it was fast moving; it was great photography to music and it was a very successful launch. So we said you know what this is a good path. The reason music was good for us was that we were a fairly young brand and so in terms of demographics we were probably the youngest in the industry after Volkswagen.[14]

Hirshberg explains:

We had done a few. That campaign was all about the realistic portraits of people in their cars having more fun than you. They were having better days than you. They were singing at the top of their lungs, they were drumming on the steering wheel. They were dressed well. They looked good. The whole goal of the ad was to say I want to be in that car with those people, listening to that music, going wherever they are going. So the first round of ads was all about people singing in their cars and they were singing the words to a song that you had never heard of which was also part of the thing as well You were hearing it for the first time. Yet the people in the ad seemed to know what it was. It implied there was some sub-culture that was cool but you didn't know about, that you wanted to find out more about. So we had done three or four of those spots with people singing in their cars. And we thought, okay, where we take it from here because it just can't be people singing in their cars campaign.[15]

Second, there was full integration starting with the album release coinciding with the commercial debut and ending with stickers on the albums. According to Hirshberg:

The sticker shows up on the outside of the CD cover. Suddenly that brand [Mitsubishi] that had very little awareness and even less pop cultural momentum suddenly had a kind of magnetism and stature that made it feel larger than life and gave it some momentum and something pop cultural that, I think, it wouldn't have had without all these things coming together... the concept of the campaign, the execution of the campaign and, of course, the music catching fire.[16]

Mitsubishi even had Dirty Vegas perform at their meetings. Gagnon says,

Dirty Vegas played at our National Theater meeting that summer, 2002, if I am not mistaken. I have never seen a group so... they were dancing, they were cheering. It was like a rock concert. This was in March. In July we had our annual business meeting. It is a big production. We introduce the next generation car and sort of tease them with future products. The finale that night was "Ladies and Gentlemen, live from coming directly from England, Dirty Vegas." I announced that and my visual of all of these people all of the sudden jumping up and dancing to the music. There must have been a thousand people there and they rolled the stage over to the people. It was one of those, wow, I am so proud to be part of this team. That was great and it was one song. They didn't have to agree to do this and they came in and did one song and then they went home. It was just amazing.[17]

It wasn't just at the Mitsubishi meetings as Hirshberg tells,

We turned these dealerships into rock concerts. It just got to such a level of coolness and currency to the brand. The best dealerships would have music like that piping through speakers and on the showroom floor and they would change the wardrobe of the guys on the floor to be a little more modern.[18]

Third, may be a little magic, or just luck, or both? "I think there is always a little X factor, a little magic. I don't know that any song would have worked. I think we kind of hit all of the right notes at one time," Shelton suggests. And Hirshberg concedes,

You know what; there is always a degree of luck whenever something catches fire. But this became a pop cultural touchstone, this became a thing. A great campaign, I think, that really changed the relationship between music and advertising forever.[19]

What is to be learned from Mitsubishi and Dirty Vegas? Why do some music in advertising campaigns work and some don't? Experts like Mike Shelton, Eric Hirschberg, Steve Smith, and Pierre Gagnon weigh in:

Music is the ultimate shortcut between an advertiser and a consumer. There is no such thing in my mind as mass media. Whether you are watching television sitting there on your couch by yourself, or with a couple of others, it is a one-on-one medium. If you give me something that I can relate to, some common ground that has already been established in my life, like music and then you intelligently connect that to what you are trying to sell me, then we've already got some common ground, a connection. Music just makes you feel a certain way. It does so much to make people feel a certain way especially when it is done right, when it is done intelligently with the right band, right track. So it is one of the most powerful devices like humor, like love, that telegraphs a certain feeling, attitude, point of view, and vibe. We are just graphing on to what already exists. And there is not a lot of other ways to do that. We are generally not picking up movie scenes or TV show scenes or quoting books or picking a lot of other stuff from pop culture because music is such a nat-ural or a medium to sight, sounds and motion. The idea behind music is it just has to be authentic, it has to fit with the narrative of the commercial, to feel like it authentically fits the brand or the product.[20]

It is one thing and one thing only for me; this is the same thing with using celebrities in commercials, its shared interest, and not borrowed interest. If the interest feels truly shared, if you can't feel the money changing hands, you don't know who got the better end of that deal. It was a great for both parties, and then that's when things like this can work. When you see certain big licensed songs in commercials you think, "He must really need the money." Because you can tell it doesn't feel right, it doesn't feel like it belongs, it feels crass. On the other hand, the concept of the ad, the kind of use of the music and the execution, are all very, very aligned, and then I think it can be great for all parties and one hand can wash to the other. The guys in Dirty Vegas, they would tell you that ad more than any marketing campaign or any traditional form of promotion was the thing that really made their careers. You look at that commercial today it could have been a music video for their song but it happened to be a music video featuring a car but it teaches organically in a way to sell natural. So I think that those are the things that need to come together: shared interest, not borrowed interest and you don't want to feel the money changing hands.[21]

I don't care how people get to the music. If that is how they get there, then that is fine. As you see, all these things that happened from that commercial, they would not have happened otherwise. Pretty much this song was dead and buried and it was most cer-tainly resurrected from that campaign. I would like to think that the song was that special but I think over $20 million for any campaign to some extent is a stick. It is wonderful, that still ten years later people have asked for the song today. It was what it was. It was a wonderful moment.[22]

1. "Music ... just has to be authentic; it has to fit with the narrative of the commercial, to feel like it authentically fits the brand or the product." Mike Shelton
2. "Shared interested, not borrowed interest and you don't want to feel the money changing hands." Eric Hirshberg
3. "Music has to match brand character. You can't pretend to be somebody you are not." Pierre Gagnon

Quote: "I can't say who but we actually got a member of the Royal Family from the UK that was a huge fan of that song. Let's just say, he has just become a Dad." Steve Smith.

Commercial Fact: "Days Go By" named one of the 10 Best Songs in Car Commercials by *Forbes* magazine (October 24, 2011)

Note: At the end of August 2011, the final Eclipse rolled off the assembly line, and was auctioned off, with the proceeds donated to charity.

"Music has to match brand character. You can't pretend to be somebody you are not."[23] Pierre Gagnon

"Days Go By"—Mitsubishi Ad Copy

'03 Eclipse. Re-mix.
Starting at $18,200
Are you in?
Mitsubishi Wake Up and Drive
Mitsubishicars.com

Songs Used in Mitsubishi TV Ads

1. "Ooh La La"—The Faces
2. "Everybody Got Their Something"—Nikka Costa

3. "Horndog"—Overseer

4. "Ladyshave"—GusGus

5. "Ballroom Blitz"—Sweet

6. "Breathe"—Telepopmusik

7. "Crazy Train"—Ozzy Osbourne

8. "Dance To The Underground" (Playground Remix)—Radio 4

9. "Days Go By"—Dirty Vegas

10. "Do You Realize?"—The Flaming Lips

11. "I See You Baby"—Groove Armada

12. "Spybreak!"—Propellerheads

13. "Superfly"—Curtis Mayfield

14. "You Get What You Give"—New Radicals

15. "In The Meantime"—Spacehog

16. "Pick Up The Pieces"—Average White Band

17. "One Week"—Barenaked Ladies

http://music.yahoo.com/blogs/yradish/songs-used-in-mitsubishi-tv-ads.html

CHAPTER 12

"Lust for Life" ... Iggy Pop and Royal Caribbean (2002)

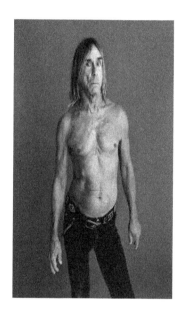

Photo by Sukita.

No discussion of popular music in advertising is complete without "Lust For Life." It is a 1977 song performed by Iggy Pop and co-written by David Bowie, featured on the album *Lust for Life*. In 2004, Rolling Stone ranked it No. 149 on their list of "The 500 Greatest Songs of All Time." And it was in a Royal Caribbean commercial. VH1 named it the 19th most inappropriate songs every used in commercials.

In one of the most egregiously woeful marriages of "whimsical activity" and "song about heroin addiction full of William S. Burroughs references and name of dead heroin dealer," Iggy Pop's

"Lust For Life" once posed undercover as an acceptable soundtrack for Royal Caribbean.[1]

Slate conducted a poll that determined that it was "the worst ad song ever."[2] So why does it make this list of the best music in advertising campaigns of all time? Because it worked. And because people are still talking about it.

In an interview with Royal Caribbean's former global sales and marketing chief, Lisa Bauer who was a big fan of Iggy Pop stated that

At the time Voyager of the Seas was coming out in 1999 and there really was an opportunity, for lack of a better word really, to be disruptive in the cruise category because at the time Royal Caribbean was announcing Voyager of the Seas with ice skating rink and the world promenade and specialty dining and a lot of firsts in innovations and the challenge was really how do you tell that story. How do you talk to a consumer about this radical departure in this cruise category? It was really about trying to undo all the myths that were associated with cruising which was cruising at the time was for *newlyweds, nearly deads*, and *overfeds*. The gist of the marketing was really around how do we talk to those that are new to cruise and even those that have cruised before to say this is really something that is completely different than anything that you have experienced or that your misperception. So we went out and we did a lot of research and we talked to consumers and you would say the name, "Royal Caribbean" and where do you go and they would go "the Caribbean," "Why?" "Because that was the name." So one of the big things really talk about the fact that, yes, we go to the Caribbean but we also go to Alaska which is what generated the Alaska spot. Yes, we go to Europe which is what generated the Europe spot. So first and foremost it was about making destinations be the hero in the ads, because we know that the number one reason that a customer picks a cruise is for the destination and the ports of call and where they can go. So that was a very purposeful part of the strategy. Then really looking at who the target audience was, the whole idea behind Iggy Pop and "Lust for Life" and get out there was around being of "explorer" mindset at the time. I want to experience new things, I want to meet new people, I want to see the world and it was all through this filter of at the time what we called and "explorer" mindset.[3]

And who suggested "Lust For Life?"

It was Arnold, out of Boston. It was a very hotly discussed topic obviously because the song is about drugs and I know Dan Hanrahan (the President and CEO) really fought, felt really strongly that it was iconic and the part that we were using of the song, "I've got a lust for life," was disruptive and clearly it was a really good decision because the campaign lasted for several years and every time that song came on, people identified it with Royal Caribbean.[4]

And what was Royal Caribbean's strategy of using popular music in their advertising, generally?

It is really about being culturally relevant and again it's obviously about the picture and what is the messaging that you are trying to talk to against your target but the use of music we often say it is something about the *motion*, the *ocean*, and *emotion*, and the music we really think is to the emotion. We had people that would tell us that they would hear the music, they would hear the bump, bump, bump and they would automatically know it was Royal

Caribbean and the would like turn around to watch. So we really do believe that ... we really see ourselves as an entertainment brand and you look at the fact that there are Broadway shows on board the ship and there's parades and there are ice shows and there's centrum-wide area artistry and so music is such a part of who we are that it just seems like it is really important piece of our marketing and our overall advertising efforts.[5]

And why was this integration of popular music in advertising excellent?

The reason I think it is excellent is because it absolutely positioned Royal Caribbean as the top brand in the category and it delivered the business results. I mean it is great if you can have the campaign advertising that you like but really at the end of the day does it make the phones ring? does it bring you the right customers stats that you want? and did it accomplish your business objectives? So, first and foremost, I would say that it really distanced the Royal Caribbean from the rest of the category. It was the combination of the introduction of the hardware with Voyagers class coupled with the propelling marketing message coupled with the fact that the ships delivered with the guests experience. It was like that perfect recipe of you told the story, the product got delivered, and the guests were happy.[6]

And what about the people who say that it was inappropriate?

I would probably say three things. First of all, most people would not even understand what the song was about and most people who would be making the issue that they were never even aware that it even talked about that. The second thing I would say is that both the actual refrain, part of it, that we used really was concentrated around the three words which was "Lust for Life," which is a very positive message and very aligned with our guests, mindset that we were looking for, that "explorer" mindset if people really wanted to get out there and experience new things. So that would be a very big piece of it, and at the end of the day people are always going to have something that they are going say no matter what you do.[7]

Iggy Pop has mentioned that he has no problem with his song being used in this manner considering it was previously getting little radio play and the commercials have sparked listener interest.[8]

1. "Be disruptive." Lisa Bauer
2. Before this campaign cruises were for *newlyweds, nearly deads,* and *overfeds.*" Lisa Bauer
3. "We often say it is something about the motion, the ocean, and emotion, and the music we really think is to the emotion." Lisa Bauer
4. "At the end of the day people are always going to have something that they are going say no matter what you do." Lisa Bauer

Iggy Pop—Lust for Life Commercial Lyrics

I'm all done, leave me, go
I'm not leaving you behind
If you guys don't quit it, I'm going to miss my massage
Here comes Johnny Yen again
Lust for life

Somewhere between the glacier hiking, the dog sledding, the train tours, and the rock wall, it hits you, this is way more than a cruise. Royal Caribbean to Alaska. Get out there.

Get out there.

CHAPTER 13

"Rock and Roll" ... Led Zeppelin and Cadillac (2002)

"Rock and Roll" by Led Zeppelin with Rolling Stones's pianist Ian Stewart is based on one of the most popular structures in *rock and roll*, the 12-bar blues progression in A. Led Zeppelin guitarist Jimmy Page later said of the song's creation:

> We were recording another number ["Four Sticks"]; we'd just finished a take and John Bonham did the drum intro and we just followed on. I started doing pretty much half of that riff you hear on *Rock n Roll* and it was just so exciting that we thought, "let's just work on this". The riff and the sequence was really immediate to those 12-bar patterns that you had in those old rock songs like Little Richard, and so on, and it was just so spur-of-the-moment the way that it just came together more or less out of nowhere.[1]

In 2002, it became one of the first famous classic rock songs to be licensed for use in a series of television ads by General Motors for their Cadillac line of automobiles called "Break Through." This was the first Led Zeppelin song used in a commercial.[2]

Jay Spenchian was former executive director of the marketing-strategy support group and now the CMO for Darden restaurants. He tells how Led Zeppelin ended up driving Cadillac:

> We were on the circuit for a while talking about the transformation in Cadillac and it [music] was a key element of it. I think there is so much emotion in music, especially classic songs. People either

remember the time of their life when those songs were played and it stirs up a lot of emotion and it bring back great memories. If it's older and they just remember the time in their lives, typically it just harkens back, it is the type of attitude that it conveys. In this case it was a more of rebellious kind attitude, it was more 180 degree counter to what you would expect from Cadillac but yet the new design was the same thing so that the marriage of the two was perfect. To move to the middle you have to do an extreme kind of thing because a lot of people don't notice. I mean if you don't do something that kind of breaks their paradigm. For every marketer, you are always looking at it and you are saying it looks different to me because I do it everyday but to the average buyer of an automobile, they wouldn't notice a difference unless it was something really really different and that's where you have to end up and to me that is what Led Zeppelin was doing for us. It was very disruptive and it was very emotional and it had the right atti- tude and it was something that you wouldn't expect. The beauty of it is that, and this is what you also do too, you worried that it was going to alienate the current 65+ core, the Cadillac Deville buyer at the time. You would worry that everybody was like that and the truth is that everyone doesn't feel their age. So these peo- ple were 65 shouldn't have seen themselves as 65 and so when you show them the ads with Led Zeppelin they loved it because it made them feel young and feel like they thought of themselves. They didn't think of themselves as older.[3]

So how did the campaign happen?

We had a bold new design for Cadillac and we were taking it in a different direction. We were really trying reinvigorating the brand and it started with kind of a vision like a lot of brands refreshing or repositioning. When you have lost a little bit of relevance, you look back in your history, look in your DNA, when you are at your best and you are at your greatest, what made you stand out, what was it about the brand that really stood out and what made it great and how would that be appropriate for the 21st Century.

So what is a modern version of what that would be? It started with design, and the design was you went to that classic 50s Cadillac, '59 Eldorado with the big fins and it was bold and it was outrageous, it was ahead of its time, and it was confident. It was things that say you are a leader and you weren't afraid to be a leader and you weren't afraid to be polarizing. Again you are in a niche business so you can't be everything to everybody. And that was GM's problem for so many years is that they tried to do cars for everyone to like a little bit versus cars that you would just love and think were great and Cadillac was great that's what it was doing. My direction was that 50s, 60s classic Cadillac look like in the 21st Century and so the new CTS was the first one that kind of came out under that design and then the next question became okay so now we have got to get some kind of break through advertising that is really going to launch. So we thought about classic rock for a lot of the reasons emotion, it is going to give it some personality, it is going to give it some energy. There is an element of bad about Cadillac, not bad, but just an element about rebelling about it that is the way that it was ultimately played out in Escalade. On the power side we were looking for that same kind of thing. We were looking at classic rock. We said okay we ought to do classic rock. We want to do something that will stir some emotions, create a point of view. Then the next piece was, never been used commercially. So we wanted to really find something that no one had ever gotten before so that people would be like, "Wow I can't believe that" So we ended up scouring all the archives and came up with "Break On Thru" by the Doors. The name of the campaign was "Break Thru." So we tested it and went through all of the testing. We really liked it, thought it was really great. We were going to do a Super Bowl ad and that is how we were going to kick off the whole campaign, "Break Thru" with the Doors "Break On Thru" and then about two weeks before Super Bowl, maybe three weeks before Super Bowl, we get a call from one of the surviving members of the Doors and he had second thoughts about selling the music commercially and just said that he was out. There were five members I think originally and so that made it three and two against. So that meant that they weren't going to be able to do it anymore because we had to have a vote of four. He was the swing vote. So he said he's out and so the Doors were out and we couldn't use that music. So here we are. We got the spot blocked for the Super Bowl and the commercial pretty much shot and so we are like all looking at each other in a conference room. I was the lead on all the product, marketing strategy and all the product launches for Cadillac and ultimately in charge of all of the communications and everything. We looked at each other and said, "What are we going to do? We have to go back scour the archive again. We have to find something really fast." So they went and found everything and came back with "It's Been a Long Time since you Rock and Roll" with Led Zeppelin. We laid it down on the commercial and everybody looked at each other and said, "Its way better. Way better, not even close." So we said, "We got to do it." That's when everybody was like this is pretty hard rock. So we did so very very quick qualitative with the current hard core older audience and they loved it too and we were feeling great about it. So we felt like okay we really have something here. It had a rebellious tone and created that emotion. I remember we kind of figured they would articulate yes, I was in high school, I was this, I was that, it was great time in my life, every time I hear that song, this is what comes to mind and its got great energy. I mean that was the biggest thing, the energy difference was like night and day. "Break Thru" was nice but it didn't have that same attitude and energy which we ultimately got from Led Zeppelin. The fact that no one could believe that Led Zeppelin would sell a song like that, was another thing. When we did it, we just felt like we really got something here and we were all pumped up about it. Ultimately that played out and it was very good because you had a built in emotional kind of point of view every time you were developing an ad. You started from a great place, it always elevated every ad. You were turning 30 percentage points just in terms of some of the measures you could get just by having it in there. Then your other message was on top of that and we used to joke around that we've got cool cars running around with great music, that's kind of the campaign. But there were other things in there again more of that kind of breaking thru attitude and just doing things a little differently, just what you would not expect from Cadillac. I mean that was the big thing is like, are you kidding me and people like Cadillac, Led Zeppelin! But the cars matched up to it and when you saw the car line up, it was like yea. There was always the one thing we did too is we torqued. Even though it was the launch of the CTS we put all of the future cars in there and so they were going to come. And we used to say it is going to be hit, after hit, after hit. So we started with CTS, and the two seat poster came out and SRX which was the sporty utility and then it was going to be the new STS and so they were all coming in cadence but we decided you know what, let's throw them all out there, which is something we never did without without a motive because everybody always worried that you are giving up the future but in this case you kind of told peo- ple we were not going to be the one hit wonders. I mean we were going to basically have a line up and you are going to see this model on to the next three or four years. That's how it happened and it's a great story. Sometimes it is better to be lucky than good. I said at the end of the day our back-up plan was an ace in the hole. It was great. It was the first time they have licensed a song. Because that was one of the things going in we saw. We wanted to make sure that it had never been licensed before. I mean we kind of thought that was important because we were really trying to send a big message that this is something new something different and we felt like if it had been associated with any other music had been associated with another product before, it would have that same impact. Robert Plant was awesome. We went to lunch with him a few times and he was tremendous, I mean he was great. Just kind of that attitude and he was the one, I think, that between him and Jimmy Page ... . Jimmy Page was a lot more open to doing it. Robert Platt was very resistant at first and really wanted to insure that he was feeling really good about it because they weren't going to take this lightly. They weren't going to just do it for anyone, you know what I mean. So we were walking through all of the things that we were going to be doing and we walked him through why we liked the song, and we walked them through we said, this is a long term deal. This is something we want to do for a long time, so this is going to be out of the signature. To this day when you hear that song a lot of people think Cadillac. We played it at every one of our meetings. It was very rallying. It inspired a lot of people. It was the right music for the right time. Like a lot of things, after I left and I think Mark was gone too they look at it and you start thinking you got to keep this campaign fresh, you got to keep it going. I always say that the agencies and the marketers are getting tired of it way faster than our consumer does. That is always the challenge. You have no data that told you. As a matter of fact there is a piece, I used to know the name off the top of my head but there was about 60% of people still didn't know we were using Led Zeppelin in our advertising. People found that hard to believe but with the purchase cycles. One thing in automotive, if you are not in the market for a car, a lot of those car commercials are noise, they just kind of go right over your head. But when you are in the market, you are all in. You are watching every car ad and you are going to the internet and you are searching and you are doing all your due diligence but if you are not in the market you don't really pay attention to it.[4]

1. "Pick a song that has a *rebellious tone* and creates *emotion*." Jay Spenchian
2. "Sometimes it is better to be lucky than good." Jay Spenchian
3. "I always say that the agencies and the marketers are getting tired of it [song] way faster than your consumer do." Jay Spenchian

Fun Fact: "Break On Thru" by The Doors was GM's first choice.

CHAPTER 14

The Silhouettes ... Various Artists and Apple (2003)

The details of "who came up with what" in the making of the iPod silhouette campaign is perhaps only known by a few insiders at Apple, its advertising agency, and contract artists. But clearly, the campaign did its job and was a smashing success. Steve Jobs and Apple, Inc. created a number of enduring cultural images with their products and marketing. And perhaps none of these is more visually memorable than the silhouette figures advertising campaign used for the iPod digital music player during the first decade of the 21st century. This series of ads—appearing in print, TV spots, and outdoor advertising—proved to be one of the most effective marketing campaigns in recent times, permeating the culture of its day and leaving its mark on the advertising industry as well. The iPod silhouette ads were particularly notable for the evocative effect they had on culture, fashion, and "hipness"— reaching Apple customers and well beyond. The distinctive marketing art used in these ads also helped Apple to sell tens of millions of iPods and also billions of songs through Apple's iTunes music store. And this advertising, in some ways, helped Apple move its business to another level, sending it in into the superstar stratosphere of the world's most elite and profitable companies. The silhouettes advertising campaign proved to be a key component in Apple's decade-long surge to the top of the world's business elite—or at the very least, became the "tipping point" campaign that put Apple on the map in a new way. The ads drew in millions of new consumers and pointed the business in a substantially new direction. For it was the simple but powerful imagery of the free-spirited dancers in these ads that helped imprint "the Apple style" around the world. The Apple silhouettes danced their way across the American cultural landscape and beyond, having a "pied piper" effect on many who saw them, sending legions straight into Apple stores and Apple websites. By 2007 Apple dropped the word "computer" from its official corporate moniker, thereafter known simply as Apple, Inc. The silhouettes advertising campaign for the iPod really didn't take hold until the fall of 2003. It was developed and coordinated by Apple's ad agency, TBWA/Chiat/Day. In the late 1960s, Lee Chiat and Guy Day formed the Chiat/Day agency in California, a firm that would later merge with TBWA in 1995. Apple began working with Chiat/Day in 1981, and the agency quickly helped Apple grow its early computer business with some famous campaigns—the 1984 "Big Brother" Superbowl TV ad, the "Think Different" campaign in 1998, and also later advertising for the iMac computer and the "Get A Mac" campaign. Lee Clow, Chiat/Day's director, became a close friend to Steve Jobs, with Jobs giving Clow and his agency the artistic freedom to design Apple campaigns. But Jobs himself often had his own ideas about advertising, and like all things at Apple, could be quite forceful in pushing his views and shaping Apple campaigns. In the case of the silhouettes campaign, however, Lee Clow's agency held its own. Sometime in 2003, the TBWA/Chiat/Day team of Lee Clow, James Vincent, a former DJ and musician, and art director Susan Alinsangan, came to a meeting at Apple with Steve Jobs to set the iPod advertising campaign. They had worked up a sampling of poster art, photographs, and outdoor billboard proposals that they spread out before Jobs on the conference room table. These samples offered a range of imagery, some of traditional photographic images on white background and others with silhouetted figures that emphasized the white iPods and their white wires. Some of the photographic images offered stills commemorating musical moments of the past which were overlain with spoken-word poems about the importance of music. Jobs was first attracted to some of the photographic images, but he saw that the ad agency team favored the silhouettes. Jobs shook his head, not certain the silhouettes would work, according to Walter Isaacson's account of the meeting in his book, *Steve Jobs*. "It doesn't show the product," said Jobs, perhaps thinking that more computer-type imagery was needed. "It doesn't say what it is." At that point, James Vincent told Jobs the silhouette images could include a tagline such as, "1,000 Songs in Your Pocket."[1] That apparently satisfied Jobs and he gave the go-ahead for the silhouettes. And as Isaacson points out, even though Jobs at first had his doubts, he was soon "claiming that it was his idea to push for the more iconic ads." In 2002, Apple had spent about $125 million on advertising for all of its products. But Jobs decided that his company might sell as many Macintosh computers by advertising iPods as it would iPods themselves. He also thought the iPod would position Apple as an innovative company and one appealing to youth. "So I moved $75 million of advertising money to the iPod, even though the category didn't justify one hundredth of that," he would later tell Walter Isaacson. "That meant that we completely dominated the [advertising] market for music players. We outspent everybody by a factor of about a hundred." In early September 2003, TBWA/Chiat/Day, launched the iPod "silhouette" ad campaign featuring anonymous black dancing figures holding white iPods with their free flowing connecting ear-bud wires, also white. The figures were cast against brightly colored backgrounds of tropical-like colors—lime green, yellow, fuchsia, bright blue, and pink. The first ads were placed on outdoor billboards in Los Angeles, California. By September 15th the ads were also running in newspapers. By October, iPod silhouette ads were appearing in music and sports magazines, and a number of others, including *Entertainment Weekly*, *MacWorld*, *Wired*, and *Newsweek*. The silhouette print ads used taglines such as "Welcome To The Digital Music Revolution" and "10,000 Songs in Your Pocket." The campaign also included posters in public places, building broadsides, and "wrap advertising" used on buses,

trains, and subway cars. The print ads were followed by TV spots
that put the same silhouetted figures in motion, each backed with
very energetic and danceable rock, pop, and hip hop music. The
first television spot featured silhouetted dancers and performers
wearing iPods while moving to the music of a group named the
Black Eyed Peas. Their song "Hey, Mama," was used in the TV
ad. The Black Eyed Peas—a hip hop/rap/pop group from Los
Angeles—were not well known at the time, and the iPod TV spot
helped improve their notice. The iPod silhouette TV spots at this
time also included the tagline, "Now for Windows" or "iPod +
iTunes." Two other TV ads followed using different groups and
their songs—"Are You Gonna Be My Girl," by Australian rock
band Jet, and another featuring "Rock Star" by N.E.R.D. The
silhouette ads soon became ubiquitous and were beginning their
rise to iconic status. Helping to do that was the sharp contrasting
imagery of the white iPod unit, white earbuds, and the connecting, free-flowing white wires. This "whiteness" turned out to be a
marketing masterstroke, focusing attention on the product in a
unique way, while also becoming an iconic part of the image. In
production, however, the white earbuds and white wires were a
happy accident, and were only white and not black because the
iPod itself was white. In the ads, it was the white color that
detailed and set off the gadget—the thing to be coveted and
acquired. One observer would later say that Apple had "stolen"
the color white—or at least hi-jacked it to good commercial
advantage. In 2003, Apple also ran versions of the silhouette ads
on the web at music sites and elsewhere, aimed in part at those
illegally downloading music, trying to coax them over to iTunes,
using taglines such as "Download Music," and "Join the Digital
Music Revolution." The silhouette TV ads featured a number of
different music genres and artists to appeal to as large a base as
possible. Some of the silhouette ads used the closing tagline "iPod
+ iTunes." The ads were soon doing as much to promote the sale
of digital music through the iTunes music store as they were the
iPods themselves. By September 2003, iTunes downloads had
surpassed 10 million songs. In October 2003, when Steve Jobs

announced the availability of Apple's iTunes-for-Windows soft-
ware and also gave a screening of the first silhouette TV ads, he
was joined in his presentation with on-screen visits from music
artists, including Mick Jagger of the Rolling Stones, Bono of U2,
and hip-hop's Dr. Dre. U2's Bono called the iPod and iTunes "a
very cool thing for musicians and music." After three months of
silhouettes advertising, iPod sales were up by 50 percent over that
of the previous quarter. In the U.S. by then, the iPod also had the
biggest market share of all MP3 players. Apple, meanwhile, was
doing a full-court press, pushing for a media "buzz effect" on its
iPod + iTunes music and marketing. By December 2003, according to one account, the Apple publicity machine has secured
6,000 iPod and iTunes stories in major publications worldwide.
Advertising Age magazine would name Apple "marketer of the
year" based largely on the success of its iPod advertising campaign. The cover of a special Ad Age report featured Apple, also
mentioning a story on the "museum styling" of Apple's brick-
and-motor retail stores, which were also coming on around that
time. By the end of 2003 Apple had sold over two million iPods,
and iTunes more than 50 million songs. In 2004, between January and August, Apple reportedly spent $49.6 million on the iPod
"silhouette" campaign, with ads and posters out everywhere.
Duke University that fall, 2004, began handing out iPods to all
incoming freshmen. One TV spot released in 2005, titled "Wild
Postings", used the silhouette style in part and was cast using
street scenes in an urban setting. The song in the ad was "Ride" by
The Vines. The ad's "story" involved a man leaving a building and
walking along an urban street, passing a wall of iPod silhouette
posters along the way. The iPod silhouette ads were by this time
familiar to many. In the TV ad, as young man passes the posters
with his iPod playing, the poster figures come to life and dance
inside their frames. But when the young man hits the stop button
on his iPod and looks around momentarily, the figures freeze,
coming to life once again as he hits "play" and resumes his walk.
Urban settings, in fact, became a particularly important part of
the iPod silhouette campaign, as billboard ads, bus kiosk posters,

building broadsides, bus and train "wraps," hanging banners, poster walls, and other forms of outdoor and "guerilla" advertising appeared throughout major cities. Outdoor advertising has gone on for decades, of course, yet Apple's silhouette campaign— featured in major cities including New York, Chicago, Los Angeles, Paris, London, Amsterdam, San Francisco, Shanghai Hong Kong, Toronto, Oska, and more—offered something of both a new look and a new intensity. Some cities were simultaneously flooded with iPod billboards, posters and banners outside, while also running print ads and TV commercials in those markets, the message being, "iPod is everywhere." iPod ads appeared in giant proportion on entire walls of huge buildings, and also in brightly-lit bus stop kiosks. In the latter case, the sharply-illuminated iPod ads in their vivid tropical colors stood out as beacons in the darkness. They offered a near luminescent quality, and could be seen at some distance, with curious, first-time onlookers no doubt drawn to them. In some cities, Apple made creative use of big spaces, as in train stations and other commuter locations. In November 2003, one blogger, reporting on the scene at Philadelphia's busy 30th Street Station of trains and subway system, noted: "There were two of those huge [wall size murals] in the lobby, and on the SEPTA platform they bought every single Viacom billboard. The Amtrak platform was also covered pretty well." By March 2004, in Paris, iPod ads were used extensively in the St-Lazare train station, where iPod silhouette banners were suspended from the ceiling every few meters. Elsewhere in the station, larger 10 foot-by-30-foot panels were used atop escalator platforms. In Amsterdam, outside the Leidsestraat station, an enormous blue iPod billboard greeted commuters as they came and went at the station. In Canada, at the McGill subway terminal in Montreal, iPod silhouette ads were practically everywhere, at ticket stands, waiting platforms, and at turnstiles. Stairways leading out of the station have also been converted into colored iPod murals, with the front of each step making up the canvas. In Toronto, building broadsides and buildings and walls adjacent to parking lots were painted with huge iPod silhouette figures. Toronto subway stations and subway cars were also painted with iPod silhouette figures. By one account, the St. George subway station in downtown Toronto in 2004 had been turned into an "Apple dreamland." Toronto resident Jonathan Ta-Min, who photographed some of the station, noted that iPod ads adorned nearly every object in the station—posts, walls, stairs, and even newspaper recycle bins. "It definitely brought a smile to my face," said Ta-Min of the iPod advertising display. In the U.K., iPod ads appeared in Virgin's music megastores, bus shelters, and throughout the London Underground. By April 2004, in Japan and France, iPod TV spots also appeared, some around the time the time the iPod mini was shipping. Back in the U.S., iPod ads appeared in subway stations and on buildings in Boston, New York, Chicago, and a number of other cities. One writer at AAPL Investors.net, who had posted photos of various iPod ads in Chicago, observed: "Chicago is a music town—hot blues, cool jazz, hard rock and many cultural varieties. So walking the town, where just about every street corner has a bus shelter, you are likely to be joined by colorful dancers groovin' to their favorite tunes...." "In ads so iconic they require no copy more than the Apple iPod logo, we get to enjoy the art. Art that makes a bus shelter or bare wall come alive. Art that makes you smile." Apple and TBWA/Chiat/Day were in effect, insinuating Apple technology into the urban tableau as both fashion and must-have "cool" technology. And their silhouette ads—from train stations and bus kiosks to magazine and TV ads—sent that message out perfectly and in some locations, incessantly, imprinting fashion and "coolness" onto the psyches of millions of potential consumers. And this was especially the case for the young. Apple's ad agency meanwhile, TBWA/Chiat/Day, soon began picking up awards for the iPod silhouette campaign. In June 2004, it won $100,000 Grand Prize Kelly Award, given to ad campaigns that demonstrate creativity and effectiveness.[2]

1. "Steve Jobs said, 'It doesn't say what it is.' At that point, James Vincent (of TBWA/Chiat/Day) told Jobs the silhouette images could include a tagline such as, '1,000 Songs in Your Pocket.' Jobs agreed." Walter Isaacson
2. "Ads so iconic they require no copy more than the Apple iPod logo." AAPL Investors.net
3. "Ad campaigns that demonstrate creativity and effectiveness." Grand Prize Kelly Award

CHAPTER 15

Angels ... Bob Dylan and Victoria's Secret (2004)

Victoria's Secret is used to getting attention ... but usually for ladies and lingerie not popular music.

"This was probably the most talked-about commercial this year," says Ed Razek, creative director of the ad and chief marketing officer for Victoria's Secret. "There was worldwide press around it." "On the basis of the impact and amount of conversation the ad got, we should have put more weight behind it," Razek says of the promotion and media buy for the ad. The ad featuring Dylan, which ran for just three weeks.[1]

Was Dylan selling out?

The Victoria's Secret ad shouldn't be a complete surprise. In fact— also in 1965—24-year-old Dylan was asked at a news conference about "selling out" as an artist. The question: "If you were going to sell out to a commercial interest, which one would you choose?" His answer: "Women's garments."[2]

And what does Razek think of Bob Dylan?

"He's an icon and gets noticed," Razek says. "And we get noticed." He admits, however, that getting noticed is not difficult, considering that most Victoria's Secret ads are slick and sultry, showing gorgeous women in underwear. "It's part of the strategy, but at least it's for a lingerie company," Razek says. "We don't sell potato chips."[3]

Ed Razek is the Chief Marketing Officer at Victoria's Secret. He tells how Bob Dylan ended up in a Victoria's Secret ad:

I did this commercial in Venice and then we tried putting all this different music against it and the commercial was quite artful. The director, French director named Dominique Grisimon was French and she had quite a European sensibility, sponsored a shot in Venice, really beautiful. We must have put a thousand pieces of music against it and nothing worked. I mean everything from Andrea Bocelli and Julio Iglesias and everybody in between, Tom Waits, everyone and nothing worked. When one of our producers found a Dylan song from *Love Sick*. I cannot remember the name of the song. It may have been called Love Sick and that was the year before. So we called Dylan's agent and he said, "You know it is funny nobody ever calls to ask if we would be interested in selling a piece of music," and I said, "Can we send you the commercial and you can take a look at it." He said, "Yea," and I sent it to him. So he called back and he said, "Bob really likes it. It is very artful, very tasteful. He really likes it. We will do the deal." And so we did. The next year I am sitting in a meeting with our Chairman, Ross Wechsler, who has the most brilliant marketing mind of anyone that I have ever met. He is kind of a legend or he is a legend, certainly a legend in the industry, but also has a great deal of vision about things and we are sitting in a meeting and he says: "Where are you shooting the Spring campaign this year?" I said, "We are going to go to Paris; we are going to shoot it, may shoot it and the Champs Elysees and so this and that." And he says, "No, go back to Venice." I am telling you exactly how it happened and I will give him full credit. I said, "Why do you think we should go back to Venice?" He said, "I think you could do more there." He said, "You only shot the one commercial there, you can certainly do more." And he said, "It seems to me that it is a good idea to continue the story." And I said, "Oh, okay, that's a good idea, makes sense." He says, "And you should use that guy again." And I said, "That guy again?" He said, "Yea, the guy that was in the commercial." And I said, "Well, there wasn't a guy in the commercial." He said, "The guy who was in the commercial." I said, "Oh, the music," and he said, "Yea." I said, "That was Bob Dylan" and he said, "You should put him in the commercial." I said, "You want me to put Bob Dylan in a Victoria's Secret commercial." And he said, "Yea, that would be cool." I know right! Yea, I wish could tell you that it came to me in a dream. I said, "I am not sure that he would do that but I will look into it." So I called his attorney back and said, "Hey, got this opportunity and you guys might want to think about it. We are going to go to Venice and shoot this spot and I know Bob liked the spot that we did last year and I wonder if he consider being in the commercial?" He says, "Nobody has ever asked him." Same thing, right, two years in a row. So I said, "Get back to us." He calls me back and he says, "He'd like to do it." This has got to be the craziest thing ever and he goes "Yea, we'll do it." I think I was in a meeting with Ross at eleven in the morning. I called the guy about 11:30 a.m. and by 12:30 p.m. I had the deal done. We went to Venice, shot with Bob and Adriana and I knew if I had Bob in the commercial I wasn't going to have army of models against him. This would be a one-on-one story. One, because of the impact of Dylan and the commercial and, two, because you didn't want to drown him in a sea of girls. You had to have a balance that aesthetically and physically worked. He sure liked Adriana. He was a little shy. He was quite professional. He was ready and willing to work with us in any way that we wanted to work. I think he was grateful that somebody asked. I think he had fun with it. He has always been kind of ahead of the crowd. When he went to the Folk Festival and pulled out the electric guitar and got booed off the stage and he was like, well, that went well. He is one of those guys. I think he would rather fall on his face than fall on his butt, meaning that if he is going to make a mistake he is going to make it on the going forward side not holding back. I think our idea to put Dylan in the commercial and then how you use that balance of Dylan against Adriana and the only time you see any reference of the two of them together because I didn't specially want to have them in the frame together because I thought it was about the pursuit of love and the frustration of love, not the realization of love. It was meant to be an isolation and if at the end she is just wearing his hat. So the whole notion of how you balance that out. I have people call me after the first time it ran and told me they literally screamed when they saw it, gasped when they saw it, they couldn't believe it. You've seen it enough that it has lost its mystery for you. You have seen it and so I have forgotten ... having done the music with Bob the year before, that having shot the commercial with Bob and then edited with Bob and with the balance of Bob with Adriana, how do you think about it, how much of Venice do you put into it, how much background, how much outside. It is all the editing decisions that you are going to have to make as you write this book. It is the same. It is all part of the creative process and it is all judgment. I think he liked it. I think he got a lot of heat about it. Candidly I am kind of more in awe of these guys as time goes on than I was when I was growing up with them but when you think of the body of work that Dylan has, the body of work that the Beatles have, the body of work that Michael Jackson had, or the Rolling Stones had. I mean giants strode the earth back then and it is like did they care about critical opinions. I think if they were looking over their shoulders they wouldn't have been the self-actualizing individuals that they were. They were writing their own rules in the same ways that Picasso and Brock kind of push each other but they weren't waiting for Art Review to come out. I think that we handled it tastefully. I think that Adriana was the perfect foil to Bob, that they balanced each other very well. Some of the other models would not have been as open in their expressions or in their accessibility. There was a vulnerability to her and an openness and a wide-eyed kind of innocence and for him there was a knowing, worldly sense of experience and I think it was the play of those two that worked so well. I mean you didn't want a model that competed with Bob. You wanted a model that complimented him and it needed to be plausible in the most innocent kind of way. We suggested nothing, with the exception of her wearing the white hat at the end. Beyond that, we suggested nothing in the spot that little movement where her one ankle rubs up against the other one. It is really a good commercial. It has every bit of residence today that it did then. I was surprised at the impact of it when I saw again now. I mean Dylan is timeless, there is no question that he is timeless. It is like Gershwin is timeless. Dylan is timeless. I think Sting is timeless and [so is] Paul Simon ... . They just had the 50th Anniversary of the Beatles, and they did that TV special and they had all of those stars, right, performing and then Ringo and Paul just blew it away. I mean they just owned it. I mean they owned it. That's incredible. All of these artists paying tribute to them and they all did a good job and I am not critiquing them but there is a reason why these guys are the icons that they are, why Dylan is the icon that he is. We couldn't have put Donovan in that commercial and made it work. Not that Donovan didn't write good music but he is not the iconic. When you look at Dylan, you know Dylan's life, you see it, you see it all there.[4]

1. "Have a balance that aesthetically and physically works." Ed Razek
2. "Dylan is timeless." Ed Razek
3. Always ask.

Victoria's Secret Ad Copy

Victoria's
Angels in Venice
Secret
I see, I see silhouettes in the window
I'll watch them 'til they're gone
And they leave me hangin' on
To a shadow.
Victoria's
The New Angels Collection
Secret

CHAPTER 16

"Love Train" ... O'Jays and Coors Light (2005)

"Love Train" was written by Kenny Gamble and Leon Huff and recorded at Sigma Sound Studios in Philadelphia by the O'Jays with MFSB. It was released on the Backstabbers album in 1972 in the United States, and reached No. 1 on the R&B Singles and the Hot 100 chart. It was certified gold by the RIAA. It was The O'Jays's first and only number-one record on the U.S. pop chart. Recorded at Philly's Sigma Sound Studios, the house band MFSB provided the backing.

Chuck Gamble is executive vice president at Philadelphia International Records and the nephew of Kenny Gamble:

> I reach out to the several ad agencies around the country and
> actually teamed up with our publisher, Warner Chapel. They

were marketing our publishing catalog to different ad agencies around the country in Chicago, New York, LA, Philadelphia, and New York. It became a good idea that what a better way to market the brand with having a family name involved, Chuck Gamble, and so we decided to join them on their presentations and then as a result we went to certain ad agencies around the country. In New York it was Platinum Rye and we gave the presentation. We presented several songs to them, which included "Ain't No Stopping Us Now," "There's a Message in the Music," "Love Train" and other hit songs for the clients they were seeking to try to land. So we played the songs for them and gave them a little background on Gamble Huff. They enjoyed the music and then in the meeting they give some idea … they didn't at the time tell us who the client was but they gave an idea of what they were thinking about in terms of Coors … and that's when we threw "Love Train" out there but frankly we thought they were going to pick "There Ain't No Stopping Us Now," to be honest with you, because we didn't know the client and they just gave us something that … in effect, it was just conceptual about a train. They weren't really clear on that and then finally they came back to us and said that they chose "Love Train" and that initially it was going to run for a six month period of time but it became so popular after they … let me back up a little bit. Before that happened, and this is pretty funny, once they identified that they were going to change the song and we worked the deal out between Sony Music and Warner Chapel, the artist, and PIR [Philadelphia International Records], because we all had a stake in this. Now they were going to use the "Love Train" sound and wanted to present it to their National Beer Convention which was very exciting … although I like Miller Lite, but it was free beer and I went. I flew to Florida to the beer convention and this beer convention was just amazing. First, everyone comes out of different meeting rooms. I guess they were testing beer and concepts about beer. Distributors were there and other folks, marketing companies were there for Coors Lite. They must have cut out about three ballrooms, two or three ballroom. When you walked in, they had the ballroom cut kind of like a Coors Lite bottle. They had it made up in there and they had dry ice as you are walking into a football stadium, bleachers on the side, two or three ballrooms. You walked in they had chicken, and pizza, and pretzels, beer kegs all along. So they really had the ambiance that they were launching a new campaign for Coors Lite and the O'Jays were there to perform and Tom Petty. They had the O'Jays performing on a stage which was shaped like a polar cap, it was really, really cool. When they did "Love Train," the people went crazy. And so after that, it was then launched and to a national campaign. Up to six months, it got a good response. They extended to another six months, and after that it comes out more like a five year campaign. And that's all she wrote. It was a very excellent campaign.[1]

Used with permission from MillerCoors LLC.

And how much did Coors pay?

I can't reveal the confidentiality of the deal. It was significant dollars between Warner Chapel, Sony and us and the O'Jays. I will say we were able to get a flat fee for each of the years that we were doing. A year at a time. As we got into year four to five, they were able to pick just certain portions of the song. They call it buttons. So we put snippets of the song. First, we were playing a portion of the song on the commercial. They were also able to brand it up very similar to the Soul Train train.[2]

What did Kenny Gamble think?

Well, in the case of Kenny, Kenny was ecstatic but we had been pushing for trying to get our music in television commercials for years. We had been in a number of commercials before this. We had had success easily with about ten or fifteen commercials, whether it be Verizon or The Gap or Old Navy or a Chevy commercial and also some success with commercials abroad, in the UK and Sweden and others and France. We were excited about this one because this one it was an American brand. Coors is up there Heineken and others in terms of branding and it was appealing to the sports brand which was a very popular brand. As Kenny got to know, that it was going to be used specifically for Coors Lite in the sports community. He knew that another audience was going to be appreciating his music and that you would hear it on the repetitive basis on TV. One, is to hear the music and appreciate the music being played and secondly, from a business standpoint we knew that the more this song would be played, there was a monetary benefits from it. From a Chapel standpoint or a recording standpoint then we knew it had some publishing value to it, that was exciting. But also for the rest of the Gamble catalog to be exposed to a whole new audience, including appreciating the great O'Jays. Sometimes African American artists are not always appreciated for their longevity and the great music that they have created. I guess for me it was a great branding tool. I am responsible for branding the company and so what a great way to brand the Gamble and Huff's name, the PIR name, and the O'Jays's name. So we could be in a position to market the catalog and increase revenue for the company.[3]

What did the O'Jays think?

The O'Jays's were thrilled, of course, they negotiated what they had, their portion of it, but they were excited. They were excited when they came to the Coors Lite Convention where they had to kick off the campaign. This is really good for them. They were very excited that day and over the years they have been excited about the use of the song. Keep in mind that, while this was happening, the O'Jays's were running the wave of another use of their songs: "For the Love of Money" in the Apprentice. Here you have a national highly rated TV series and then you have one of the very popular commercials.[4]

And what did this mean for Philadelphia International Records?

It was the transition from being just a record label to entertainment company to a branding company and to refocus our efforts to generate new revenue for a catalog that had been around at that point, for 30 years. So we didn't fear selling out frankly because we saw this as evolution of how music ... the extension of time of music, the extension of great songs that can be used in different platforms. Here we have today the platforms have expanded to so many other areas including games and other areas. I would think no one considers it a sell out when you have a platform using music written 30 years ago and if it wasn't for these platforms such as television filming commercial these songs could be dead.[5]

1. Proaction can be better than reaction when trying to place music in advertising.
2. "Exposure to a whole new audience." Chuck Gamble
3. "Extension of time of music. Extension of great songs." Chuck Gamble

CHAPTER 17

"Back in Black" ... AC/DC and The Gap (2006)

The press release from the Gap read:

> This week, the skinny black pant is back at Gap with the introduc-
> tion of a new, groundbreaking campaign featuring original film
> footage of timeless style icon Audrey Hepburn. The campaign,
> entitled "Keep It Simple," is centered on innovative television
> spots incorporating a memorable scene of Audrey Hepburn danc-
> ing in the classic film *Funny Face*. Celebrating Gap's relaunch of
> the perfect black pant, the ads mark Gap's third and final market-
> ing campaign of the fall season. "Gap has a rich history of inte-
> grating memorable choreography and music into our advertising,
> but we've never done anything quite like this before," said Trey
> Laird, creative director of Gap. "We wanted to do something
> really special to relaunch our skinny black pants and thought
> who better to showcase them than actress Audrey Hepburn—an
> iconic woman famous for dressing with sophistication and clas-
> sic style." Debuting September 7, Gap's new "Keep It Simple"
> TV spots juxtapose classic footage of Audrey Hepburn dancing in
> skinny black pants to the 1980 AC/DC hit song "Back in Black."
> The ad opens with a scene from *Funny Face* as Audrey Hepburn
> dances through a Parisian cafe. It continues as she jumps out of
> the movie and onto a backdrop resembling the look and feel of
> an iconic Gap ad. Special effects and graphics help her navigate
> her way across the screen in a series of energetic dance steps. She
> then jumps back into *Funny Face* as the spot concludes with the
> tagline "It's Back—The Skinny Black Pant." The "Keep It Sim-
> ple" television campaign features 30 and 60-second spots that will

air in the United States on all major networks, spot markets and cable from September 7 through October 5. The spots will premiere on network television shows including "Grey's Anatomy" (ABC), "CSI" (CBS), and "Studio 60" (NBC). Gap.com will also feature the new "Keep It Simple" television commercial, as well as exclusive, behind-the-scenes footage of the making of the ad. Complimenting this outstanding broadcast effort are a series of black-and-white print ads featuring models in clean, simple looks anchored in skinny black pants will run in October issues of major national magazines including *Vogue*, *InStyle*, and *Elle*. There will also be outdoor ads in major markets. Laird + Partners, Gap's creative agency, developed the "Keep It Simple" marketing campaign. The TV spots were developed using visual effects by Method Studios and graphic design and animation by Logan and print ads were photographed by famed fashion photographers Inez van Lamsweerde and Vinoodh Matadin. In celebration of the launch of the "Keep It Simple" ad campaign, Gap is making a generous contribution to the Audrey Hepburn Children's Fund. The Audrey Hepburn Children's Fund is a nonprofit organization created to continue Ms. Hepburn's international appeals on behalf of children around the world.[1]

The *Los Angeles Times* reported:

You just can't keep a good woman down. Audrey Hepburn has returned from the Other Side this month and is starring in an ad campaign for Gap, the struggling retailer that is pinning its hopes on the actress, who died of colon cancer in 1993. She joins many dead colleagues—Fred Astaire (Dirt Devil), John Wayne (Coors) and Humphrey Bogart (Diet Coke)—in her posthumous marketing career. The Gap spot is based on a clip from the 1957 romantic comedy *Funny Face*. Hepburn plays a clerk in New York who is discovered by a fashion photographer (Astaire) and whisked off to Paris to take the fashion world by storm. (No stretch, really, given her real-life role as muse to the French designer Hubert de Givenchy.) In the ad, Hepburn, in a black turtleneck and black pants, is shown leaping from her chair in a Paris nightclub, exclaiming, "I rather feel like expressing myself now. And I could certainly use the release." She starts a goofy Bohemian dance, then springs from the frame onto a white background as the AC/DC song "Back in Black" blares. Some love the spot; some are appalled that a dead Hollywood icon is being used to sell skinny black pants. "The Gap should be ashamed of themselves," wrote one commenter on ThirdWay Advertising Blog. "It's a desperate attempt by a desperate company to align itself with someone classy." "I wanted to like it," posted another, "but at the end was just too offended by the reincarnation of Audrey Hepburn as a pants salesman." Gap, for its part, is happy just to be back on people's minds. For the last two years, the company has failed to excite customers who have fled elsewhere for inexpensive basics. Reviving a staple like the slim black pants, part of its new "Keep It Simple" campaign, could help revive Gap's sliding fortunes. Steven Levitt, who created Q scores, which measure name recognition and the likability of celebrities, said he thinks the choice of Hepburn is "excellent." "If it's executed in good taste, her appeal will carry the advertising very well," said Levitt, president of Marketing Evaluations, Inc. Every two years, his firm conducts a survey to determine the Q ratings of 168 dead celebrities. In the most recent one, Hepburn ranked in popularity behind only two other women—Lucille Ball and Katharine Hepburn. "If you started searching for a likable female with strong recognition to a current female audience," said Levitt, "Audrey Hepburn would be the first one you'd come to. Lucille Ball would represent comedy, and Katharine Hepburn would probably have a much older skew." Audrey Hepburn's son, Sean Ferrer, approved the ad and worked with the company on the spot. "We ran everything by him, and he had lots of things to say," said Andrew. With her wide eyes, graceful neck and boyish figure, Audrey Hepburn has been a fashion icon nearly since she was plucked from a crowd in 1951 by the novelist Colette to star in the Broadway adaptation of "Gigi." As a teen, she suffered malnutrition while living in Nazi-occupied Holland, and was always reed slender. At 5 feet, 7 inches tall and

110 pounds, she could easily get away with skinny black pants. But is anyone buying? "We've seen a lot of positive signs," said Andrew. "We're very happy."[2]

Kyle Andrew, formerly VP of Marketing at The Gap and now Senior Vice President, Marketing at Kate Spade, New York, said about the campaign at the time:

"We're thrilled because this is the first time in more than 12 years that a film clip of Audrey Hepburn has been authorized to endorse a commercial product in North America," said Kyle Andrew, vice president of Gap Marketing. "This ad is a true testament to timeless style and we couldn't be more excited to have Audrey Hepburn—the ultimate style icon—represented in our campaign."[3]

The campaign received a lot of reaction both positive and negative, to which Andrew responded at the time:

"The worst thing a marketer can do is spend a lot of money and people are like, 'Oh well, another ad for Gap,'" said Kyle Andrew, Gap's vice president of marketing. "This is polarizing. Any time we can do anything that elicits passion is great."[4]

Steve Scharf, CEO of Steven Scharf Entertainment said of the campaign:

We publish AC/DC, they are the most expensive band in the world to license. The Gap came to us. They had this concept of Audrey Hepburn wearing black, you know, dancing. It was a pretty no brainer that Back in Black would be a great. We had to get approval. We administer their [AC/DC] publishing. They own their publishing and their masters. They control their career very tightly and they are very very picky about what they license and what they don't license. The say no more than they say yes and that was one that they really liked. They saw the story boards and they really dug it. The band makes the final call. TV has become the new radio. When artists started to break by more records from having placed in some television shows that really changed the landscape. The revenue is tremendous. Very few artists get to be on hit radio. Unless you have a major label behind you or are a big independent that's got use of radio. I really felt that this placement was very synchronistic as you had an iconic figure of Audrey Hepburn from the Fifties dancing in her blacks coupled with and iconic song from AC/DC with "Back in Black." The image and the music were an outstanding match![5]

1. "The worst thing a marketer can do is spend a lot of money and people are like, 'Oh well, another ad.'" Kyle Andrew
2. "TV is the new Radio." Steve Scharf

CHAPTER 18

"The Hamsters" … Various Artists and Kia (2008)

In 2008, Kia unveiled its new "Soul," it released the "Hamsters." It was a five-part campaign called "A New Way to Roll" and created by Los Angeles-based ad agency, David & Goliath (see Figures 18.1–18.5). The first ad depicted

> a computer-generated Levittown populated by giant hamsters. As the rodents spin in place on their hamster wheels, waiting for the traffic light to change, the drudgery of their gridlocked exercise is suddenly interrupted by the arrival of a red Kia Soul. When the car pulls up to the intersection, the passenger-side window rolls down to reveal a posse of three hipster hamsters who are clearly enjoying their ride.[1]

This first campaign also played four different artists and songs each time the window opened: "Do What You Do" by Marz, "Fort Knox"

Figure 18.1 2009: "A New Way to Roll"

Figure 18.2 2010: The choice is yours featuring Black Sheep's "This or That"

Figure 18.3 2011: Share some soul featuring LMFAO's "Party Rock Anthem"

by Goldfish, "Junkyard" by The Potbelleez, and "Colours" by Calvin Harris. The four commercials that followed featured: "The Choice Is Yours (Revisited)" by Black Sheep, "Applause" by Lady Gaga, "Party Rock Anthem" by LMFAO, and "In My Mind (Axwell Remix)" by Ivan Gough and Feenixpawl featuring Georgi Kay.

Michael Sprague is the executive vice president of Marketing and Communications for Kia Motors America (KMA) where he oversees all aspects of the marketing and communications departments, including:

Figure 18.4 2012: "Bringing Down the House"

Figure 18.5 2013: "Totally Transformed"

brand marketing, advertising, retail marketing, sponsorships, Customer Relationship Management (CRM), corporate planning, and public relations. He tells the story of how the wheels began to turn:

> The origins of the campaign go back to Fall 2008 because we were getting ready to launch the new Soul in March of 2009. Up until that point the brand was basically known for a cheap and cheerful product. It was a fuel efficient, below cost and non-descript

product that served as basic transportation for people. The Soul was the first vehicle that was going to kind of lead of our brand transformation of the product, the product line transformation so the Soul was the first out of the box. I had just joined the company in August of 2008. So this was kind of a first launch, one of nine over a three year period. And the agency [David & Goliath] came in on October 31st, Halloween, dressed in their Halloween costumes, and pitched us on a couple of ideas. We had written the marketing brief and the creative brief came out of that. The insight behind it were we had worked with a small consulting company that focused on youth in terms of what the Gen-Y customer thinks in terms of the need toward music, and gaming, and their friends, and the social aspect of their lives, things along those lines. The agency came in and pitched a couple of ideas. It actually came down to two ideas that the team, my team, would split on. Obviously one was the Hamsters which ultimately got the nod but the other one got around the idea the inspiration for the product came from one of our designers here in the U.S. He was in Korea and he was watching a documentary, one of these nature shows, like the Discovery channel or something of this sort. It was on boars, the wild animal boars, and he started sketching a boar and then he put a back pack on the boar and that kind of became the inspiration for the design of the Soul which launched back in 2009. The second idea was around the idea of a boar with a back pack and thank God we went with the Hamsters. We needed to make a big splash in the marketing place with this product. At the time we were about 1.9% market share player and we are now at 3.8%. So it doubled our market share over the last five years. Not just because of the Soul but because of all of the other products that have supported and come after that. So we were being totally outspent, out-smarted outside the given marketing place. Our awareness back in December, 2008 was 54% and now it is 63%, so up 16.7%. Our familiarity, for those who are aware of the brand, people who are actually familiar with us, it was 14% in December 2008. We are now at 23% so up 64% there. Opinion went from 38% to 60% with consideration among those who are aware went from 34% to 58%. So in the last five years we have had pretty good movement in our upper funnel metric. But back to the Soul. Out spent, out shouted and people didn't know who we were; often confused with the Ikea brand. So that just kind of shows you what the market place was. Also, as we were preparing to launch in March 2009 it was late 2008, the economy was just a disaster, people were losing their jobs, closing plants, all of those types of things and so we basically rolled the dice and said here's a really fun car that we think is going to be perfect for the marketplace. I guess people were looking to downsize in what they had because of the economy and gas prices and we needed to kind of take a fun approach to it. As a brand, we wanted to challenge traditional automotive convention in terms of when you introduce a new car you show it on a nice windy road, leaves blowing, beautiful shots of the car and here it is. We wanted to completely go against and say, hey, let's tell a story and let's do it in a fun way. The hamsters serve as kind of the metaphor for people who living the everyday life, the routine of the every day life and they are looking to get off of that routine and get out of the traditional vanilla econo-boxes that permeated the marketplace back then. The first the campaign was "The New Way to Roll" and we introduced a vehicle with four different up and coming bands. One was Goldfish. What we did was every time the hamster rolled down the window and kind of nodded his head, we had different music. We had four rotations, four spots that rotated four songs. So when you are watching it on broadcast you weren't really sure which music you would hear until the window came down. So that is how we got some initial social buzz out of it. Blacksheep was the following year, that's when the campaign kind of really took off. That was when we were comparing ourselves, but not directly again, using the toasters, cardboard boxes, and washers which represented some of our competition using the Blacksheep song: "You Can Go With This," meaning our Soul or "You Can Go With That," meaning toasters, cardboard boxes, and washers. [The song] really had popularity back in I think the early 90's and here we brought it back, it connected with people who remember it from those days and also connected with a new generation of listeners that connected to it. They loved the creative and music as well.[2]

When asked about the role of popular music in Kia advertising, Sprague said:

It goes back to the initial insight that we got from research that the target that we were going after was Gen-Y, particularly the Gen-Y male. We knew that music was such a huge part of their lives. The iPhones had just come out a year or two earlier. Prior to that we all had the minis and before that there were all of these devices with music and music was with them everywhere. So we always go back to that as kind of the foundation for why we continue to have music a big part of the Soul campaign. There is also that emotional connection that music helps make to the car and to the spot and to the brand, it helps keep it all together. We have now integrated pop culture into the spots as well. With the Lady Gaga you see the slimmed down hamsters and that is kind of a nod to what is going on in society these days where people are trying to look thinner, working out more, trying to look fitter. Slim fit suits are becoming hugely popular. People are trying to show off their bodies, more stylish hair. You see it in Hollywood and now it is permeating throughout across the country. We try to look at what is about to become popular and weave those into the campaign as well. So back in 2011, when we did the LMFAO "Party-rock Anthem" that is when some of the gaming companies were getting ready to release their biggest games ever like "Minecraft" and "War of the World." Gaming was so big and that's why that whole look and feel with the Soul spot "Party Rock Anthem" with LMFAO had that whole look and feel of a game. The 2012 "Bringing Down the House" that was the nod towards electronic dance music. We've seen again through research and through our agency who really seems to have a pulse or the finger on the pulse of pop culture came to us and said this is going to be big this year, this is what we want to do from a music standpoint and so that's how we ended up there. In March 2009 we launched the Soul and we went on to launch other products as well. Traditional automotive convention is that you launch a product for three, six months maybe, and then you kind of move on and you never go back because you are always looking forward to launching new products. The Soul was well received by the media, our consumers, and our dealers and they said let's do another campaign. We've got this property, this partnership with MTV and let's use that as a platform to launch our new campaign. So we did the second spot that was in June of 2010. We had a partnership with the VMAs, Video Music Awards. Sales took off and the campaign became hugely popular and so we thought we should do this every year. So basically every year for five years we have had a pretty significant campaign built around the Soul. We haven't done that with any other products at all, any other brands that would have followed suit with that. And it has now become our number two selling vehicle. When we were first going to market, we forecasted in our best year, we would proba-bly sell about 50 to 60 thousand vehicles and since 2011 we have consistently sold over 100,000. The campaign is definitely having build awareness for the vehicle and for the brand. The product just turned to be really cool and very relevant for the times and it connecting with the younger buyer who we are targeting but a lot of people, particularly older people are buying it as well. When we talk to them, it is for two reasons: (1) They like the imagery that the Soul says about them, they are young, they are hip, they are connected, they understand, they can talk to their kids and their grandkids because as grandparents, they still want to be perceived as connected with their kids and their grandkids but also it has great functionality, it seats five, cargo, the whole bit. (2) The youth tell us they are buying it because of the imagery, they think it's cool but really the technology in the vehicle and the design of it. So we are connecting two very different audiences with the vehicle.[3]

When asked if artists are now coming to Kia, Sprague said:

We definitely get more solicitations from everybody, not just music but movies. Five years ago I was begging people to consider me, "hey, take a look at our products" and they were like, "no thanks." Now because we have had some success we are definitely being sought out much more often. Antidotally, somebody claiming to represent Justin Bieber sent an email last week saying he has a new video coming out and he really wants a Kia Forte to be in the video. I always look at these things with somewhat of a jaded eye, having been in the business for a while. Usually they are coming to us because they want us to spend a lot of money to put my product in their video, as a product placement. We take the approach that we are not going to pay for that. We have had some success with that in the past, and we have had others that weren't so successful and so we kind of just take the approach of if you want our cars we are happy to give them to you but we weren't not going to spend money and put them unless it is part of a media buy where it is built into the story. Other brands take a much different approach.[4]

Colin Jeffery is the executive creative Director and Managing Partner of David & Goliath. He adds to the animal tale:

Where it started and it has come a long way over the last six years, and going back kind of to the generation where it started, we were tasked with promoting the Soul which is this new vehicle that obviously was very boxy and had a very distinctive look to it. At the time, six years ago now, and the Scion on really had monopoly on the boxy car market with their Scion XB and had a very passionate following. Obviously, did a lot of homework on the category and the advertising around Scion XB and they had a monopoly not only on the boxy market but also on the car, look and feel, the creative work that supported it. Definitely there were very street and gritty and graffiti and tattoos. It was trying very hard to be cool, and obviously they had done a good job with that because they were selling a lot of cars and they had this sort of passionate following and they owned that space. We were launching at the same time, or pretty much the same time line, launching the cube and there were two ways to go you could just kind of follow the trend and do more of the same and jump in with the graffiti and the tattoos and try and be cool. I had a feeling that Nissan may go down that same path and I just didn't want to get stuck me too category and just kind of blend in. So we went about creating work that looked and felt distinctly different to anything out there and we really landed on the strategic idea of first which is "A New Way to Roll" and come up with idea that as humans, we kind of get stuck in the daily grind in our routine and we just kind of tend to do the same things that are comfortable and we buy the same products and we go to work, sit in our cars in traffic, and we just kind of go through the motions and we get stuck in this wheel, right. And Kia being this new innovative brand and the car being very distinctive gave you an option, right, something new, something different. It was never really about screwing the system or counter-culture. It was really that we are all facing the same challenges and we go through life in the same way. You have a choice. There are different ways to do it. You can be boring, doing the same as everyone else and do the expected or you can try a new way to roll. The first idea was really just coming up with hamster wheel, where everybody's stuck. The first one really set the scene where the hamsters are stuck on freeways and the wheel going round and round and round actually going nowhere. So that is where it came from, kind of going through the daily grind, struck in a routine and then in comes this new shiny red, distinctive looking vehicle with the cool hamster in, the window comes down and they just have found an alternative. So, that is really kind of where the whole campaign stems from and we did a really interesting thing with the first ad. I think it is the first time it has ever been done is we actually finished it with four different music tracks and so every time the window came down in the car, the hamsters are listening to different pieces of music. And that was purposely done. At the time, and still today, we realized there is a generation that loved discovery. You want to be discovering new music and once everybody is listening to the same band, the same music, you are no longer cool. You all want to be cool, you want to kind of be cutting edge and have music on your iPod that your friends don't have, right. So for that first one, when we purposely chose bands that are on the fringe or up and coming and bands that were very universal and we purposely put four into rotations to create an online debate. So, we used four bands for the first one; the first band was Calvin Harris from Scotland and has since become a huge name in the states. Goldfish from South Africa who must have done really well there, they have been a house band there at a plush nightclub and have been there for the past six or seven years now, toured with Basement Jaxx and a bunch of big, big bands. The Pop Belly from Australia and Marz from Chicago. A few of them were bands that we had been tracking for a while. Goldfish on the Seas, an African band which I know well and was really tracking them and they were kind of poised to do really well. It worked on two levels. It honestly helped us because it was a band that had a cool factor and were on their way up and then two, we really used this campaign to introduce people to different songs that they may not have heard. So it is kind of mutually beneficial and so we used it to help push music that we believed in or liked. So it gave them a really nice leg up. In fact, at the end of the year, they finished in the top ten dance albums of iTunes in the US and they had almost no presence here before the campaign. I got a great note from the guys in the band going "Hey do you think that little campaign had anything to do with our success in the US?" This was cool and, of course, Calvin Harris, obviously he was on the college tour here and he was just starting to break through and has done well. Marz is just something we just found and liked. Some of it was just from tracking and monitoring bands and some were just ones we found and felt it would fit the mix. The beauty of it and it really worked well is, so imagine you watch the commercial for the first time and you see the window come down and you hear the band Calvin Harris and you go online and watch it and there are people commenting on YouTube and you think Calvin Harris but I am watching the next day and I see the ad with Goldfish and I see your column saying it was Calvin Harris and I am like, no, it was not Colin Harris, it was the Potbellies. So we kind of created this online debate. It took a while for people to get the fact that we had a bunch of different ones in rotation. So it created this really interesting online debate and at the same time was educating people when they were introducing them to different songs. It's interesting and I am not sure it has ever been done before since but definitely it was effective and kind of made Kia cooler. I think it made people believe we had our finger on the pulse.[5]

As to the idea creation, Jeffery said:

I think we did come up with the idea and saw like the strategic platform "New Way to Roll" that was first and then the music, I mean you obviously want to connect with the audience and we wanted to do it in our own way. So music was important from the outset but we didn't know how we would use music at the gate. It evolved in the event that we developed the strategic platform. I think it was important to us not to do the expected. You could have always opted to have used a giant popular band and just paid tons of money and whack it on your commercial and hope for the best. We very strategically used up and coming bands because it suited the introduction of the new car, new band, new songs, new cars, new look. My take on this stuff is when you sit down I stay very close to open labels and senior execs at the various labels and try to keep a finger on the pulse and stay in contact with them and just know what is happening in the music space and one of the things that is usually important to us as an agency in keeping the integrity of the music in tack. I have a major issue with just buying the hot new song and schlepping on a shitty piece of work. It doesn't do any good for music and to me the single most successful thing is when they are mutually beneficial. I feel like we are in a position as clients and an agency where you can help to promote the music and you can push the music and at the same time the artist through social media, through their following and through the song can help make your brand better. It seems in poor taste when you see an awful ad with like an amazing track of some leg-endary artist and in your mind you just go, how much are they paying for that because the ad sucks and the song is great and it all kind of ends up hurting the artist and that to me is not good. I think if you grew up in 70's, 80's and even the 90's, it was kind of as a band you didn't sellout, you kept it real and if that meant not doing any commercial. I think today this generation understands and accepts the fact that for their favorite band this is one great way to promote music and get it out there, I think, this generation is accepting of that. You have such a small window now with music, music being disposable, in a way, everything just comes and goes so quickly that you have that little window where you are popular and you have time to make some money and make a name in the industry. I think this generation is a little more accepting of the fact that you put your music in advertising and as long as it is good creative work, everybody wins. I think even the fans are cool with it. The campaign obviously then took on a life of its own, it just evolved and every time we had to do something new, whether it was "A New Way to Roll" or not, it is how you keep this thing fresh. The challenge changed every time so that by the time we launched the second campaign which was the Black Sheep, "The Choice is Yours" We got to the point where we decided to just overtly take on the competition but in the first one was really positioning ourselves as "A New Way to Roll" was an alternative and the second campaign installment was let's just overtly take on the competition. We did that in a way that the younger generation would understand. I think there are certain names on the street that people have for these various cars so we used kind of metaphors to take on the competition so you can get with us or you can get with that and we showed kids in a toaster which is a street name for some of the other boxy cars and the washing machine which is another street name one of the other boxy cars. So you still have driving toasters and washing machines but between all of the generations you would kind of be like it's cute and bizarre but to our core audience they understood exactly what we were saying. The music, we decided to go to something old school because again it worked from two levels. You have the audience, you have the younger core audience that is all about discovery and then because it was an old song it had nostalgia for like the older audience who were buying this car. We loved the fact that the song to anyone in their twenties would be brand new and it is still a bad ass track but it is actually an old song and it was kind of an interesting place where we were with music. Something old can be new to this younger generation and they love discovery, so we threw it out there and it was a huge successful for us. Kids jumped on it and they loved it, and it made total sense conceptually. You can get this as in Kia Soul or you can get with that as with the toaster and washing machine. So we went into that world which is a little more kind of hip-hop and the streets and we designed the wardrobe and the whole vibe around it that which is great and it worked very well for us. After that we had to go somewhere else again and just staying close to labels and people like Steve Berman and Jennifer Thornburg at Interscope Records. I got to listen this single "Party Rock," and it hadn't even been released in the US yet and so I was with them and they played me this new track from LMFAO. I heard it and I was like straight away just had this feeling that it was going to be the biggest song in the world. So I raced off to Kia and we were working on the next commercial already and I went down to them and I said, "guys we have to hear the song, trust me it is going to be the biggest song in the world." And they were like, how do you know and I am, just trust me I have a feeling this has it. It has everything you really need. It is positive; it is colorful; it is fun; it has a good message. It had be released in Canada. They were beginning to get some traction in Canada. So we sat down with Interscope and locked the track up. We got the track early. We were lucky that that one would work well for us. Conceptually, we were somewhere else with this one. So we had done the street thing. We had done the direct competition, overtly taking on the sounds and the key to the world. So what should we take on next? The world was kind of in a bad place at the time, just hard-hit with the recession on, and a lot of violence, it was a somber time globally. So we thought that this little car, it is kind of a way of life, it is bright and it is colorful and it is cute and it just pushed positivity. At the same time gaming is such a big thing and it kind of sucks because kids sit in front of a computer in dark rooms or in front of a TV and just play games and shoot each other. So it was kind of this whole thing like the world is in a bad place and there is a lot of violence out there and kids are just sitting in the dark playing video games instead of getting out and just driving and seeing the world. So how do we take this and put a positive spin on it. At the same time LMFAO was doing the same thing with "Party Rock," it's about self-expression and getting out there and having fun and just being an individual, bracing life in the summer. So it all worked very well conceptually. Actually from that commercial we open in the first world futuristic type environment with guns and shoot-ing and explosions and then through music and with this bright, lively little car, you get everyone to put down their arms and obvi-ously dance and so everyone is doing the shuffle and it becomes kind of a big colorful dance party. So the message was lay down your weapons and have fun and get out there and express yourself, have fun. It really just became more of a high level message of just promoting self-expression and color and just have fun, don't take yourself too seriously. It became one of the most viewed commer-cials on the television of all time and unfortunately our licensing ran out in a few months, eight months ago and so we were around 30 million views and still climbing with about a million views a month. When we took it down, it was just sad. For Kia it was one of the five most viewed commercials of all time. It was definitely way up there and hugely successful song, and sold a record amount of cars and it created a major following for the Hamsters. We had also developed a clothing line for the hamster and so Hamstar which you see them wearing in all the ads, they have their own line of clothing and we actually developed the full blown e-commerce site as well which is hamsterclothing.com and we still sell a fair amount of merchandise through that as well. From there we moved to fourth installment. The whole Electronic Dance Music (EDM) movement was really starting to take off and we thought that might be an interesting segway place to play. So we looked at a bunch of music and we really started looking at who was doing what and a little worried that those might be too expected or that other people might jump on them because it was beginning to get traction. We found the track "In My Mind" a Feenixpawl track. We started in Prague and it was really kind of made to feel like old world and there was this classic opera and theatre and it is kind of this old stuffy environment and we go in there and we kind of shake things up again and introduce color and electronic music to kind of a seemingly old stuffy world. And again just promoting "This New Way to Role" message where you don't have to get stuck in the old ways, let's keep moving this thing forward and we noticed something really interesting happening in music. You were seeing a lot of old songs so classical music, folk, different sounds being mixed with an electronic. So that was another interesting thing we saw. Well, let's take this song and then re-score it with classical and do our own rendition of it and so you see in there we brought in all of these strings and we made a kind of really beautiful classical composition and that was the trend we were seeing in electronic music at the time and still today. The fifth which is our most recent. We have to do something new again. The good thing for us is we have a new vehicle but the car itself is new, it has been redesigned and so it was slicker, more sophisticated, lots of new cool technology, heat and cool seats and on-board entertainment system and lots of gadgets and just slicker lines and just more refined. It is just slicker and more sophisticated, and so maybe it is time we got these guys looking slick and sophisticated like the car and it obviously helps for us with the whole color, suit and tie, mood interest was big in the celebrity world at the time, lots of artist kind of doing that, going back to kind of the rat-pack look, the jelled hair and the skinny European suits and the bow ties, that whole thing was very popular. We obviously wanted to ride that a bit and at the same time we decided let's just blow this thing out of its time, let's just go full-on mainstream with it and we looked at a lot of music and then again through our relationships with the labels and Lady Gaga was working on "Art Pop" and we heard "Applause" and it just figured to be true. She is amazing. She has got a great following. She hasn't released anything in a while which I think there was a lot of anticipation around "Art Pop" and she is all about self-expression. You work very well for us in terms of the two brands aligning. It was a message of a song was bang on for us and we had the idea first obviously this idea of sophisticated, more refined, sleeker, skinny down the hamsters and then that piece of music just really brought the whole thing to life and it was just a perfect song for us and she was great about it. She is another artist that truly understands marketing and social media and she was great. She got aboard and tweeted about it. I think because she honestly like the creative she was happy to get involved. It wasn't part of the deal. She didn't have to do any social media for us, she just genuinely liked it and then obviously she's got an big voice in social media and that definitely helped us. I'd like to think that we helped promote the song at the same time.[6]

1. "There is that emotional connection that music helps make to the car and to the spot and to the brand, it helps keep it all together." Michael Sprague
2. "You obviously want to connect with the audience and do it in your own way. Music was important from the outset." Colin Jeffery
3. "It is important to keep the integrity of the music in tack." Colin Jeffery

CHAPTER 19

"Lose Yourself" ... Eminem and Chrysler (2011)

Eminem doesn't license his music, or at least not "Lose Yourself."

Over the past decade, rap legend Eminem has been approached over 100 times to license his classic "Lose Yourself." Up until now, he has refused all bidders, turning down millions of dollars along the way, according to Joel Martin, who controls the Eminem music catalog and has one-third of the writing credit on the song. But that was until Chrysler chief marketing officer Olivier Francois started selling Martin on how much he wanted the music, and how he had an idea to show off Detroit to the Super Bowl audience, the largest TV audience of the year.[1]

Eminem felt very strongly about Detroit. "The city of Detroit is really important to Marshall," says Martin. "Two years ago, Marshall was down for the count, and he understands what Chrysler is trying to do."[2] In 2009, Eminem released "Relapse" to a lukewarm reception and many felt that he was done making hits, ironically the same year that Chrysler was force in bankruptcy and needed a bailout from the Federal government. Francois used all this to his advantage to get the song he wanted from the Detroit born and raised Eminem. "I felt very strongly about this piece of music and Eminem," says Francois. "I don't believe in using celebrities and famous people just for the sake of it. Their story has to make sense in the story of the ad."[3] This is the story:

> I have this song in my head because somebody on my team, Tim Kuniskis, who was my right hand at the time at Chrysler and then became the head of Fiat of America when I took over the responsibility as being the head of Fiat Worldwide, was really obsessed with this "Lose Yourself" song. So he brought it to my attention and then we started thinking about this song and quoting the song and in my speeches. I had this "Lose Yourself" song coming from my buddy and colleague, Tim. And so that's how the idea started, let's use the song from commercial, "imported from Detroit commercial." So I have a lot of connections with the music industry in California, in LA and even in New York. I am a former music producer and so that is what I was doing before, years ago, before being in the automotive industry. From these old times, so I have a lot of connections with the music industry especially in LA and I am a very close friend with Jimmy Iovine, as an example, and people at Universal and so I started calling them and saying look I need your help, I need to connect with Eminem and the funny thing is that I knew that Eminem was Detroit-based because that is exactly why he interests us but I have been looking for him through LA, through very remote, very distant connections while actually he was just here, a few miles from here [Detroit] and so I had this connection with his musicians from Detroit. But I didn't connect the dots by mistake, I connected him to LA, while all I had to do is connect him to Detroit. And so these relationships, you know, he has a publisher and his publisher owns a studio and his name is Joel Martin and the studio is in Ferndale [Detroit]. I had no phone number I just had an address and we were in December just after the Auto Show. So there was a lot of snow and I was very concerned you know when you are really very worried because I secured these two minutes of Super Bowl and it was a huge financial commitment, a huge responsibility, and I committed to two minutes at the Super Bowl and I had no plan B.

The only idea was this Eminem "Lose Yourself" idea. And I could not make it happen; I could not get hold of him because I didn't have the connection. I had this indication of a studio. So I drive there at night, really night time, it was like 9 or 10 pm. So I take my truck actually, it was a pick up, Ram, four-wheel drive because that is what you need in Detroit. I knocked at the door and there was some two or three feet of snow and the miracle was he opened. It was my lucky day because it was like 10 pm at night and I knock at the door. There was no sign, there is nothing telling you it was a studio. You are in the Detroit suburb at night and in a very lonely trip and the door opening, that's Joel Martin and I guess that he probably thought that I was kind of crazy for a few minutes. I mean you knock at the door claiming you are the CEO of Chrysler. He probably thought that I was totally... But then okay, that guy opened the door connected me with Eminem's manager, as well, with Eminem in person and made it work. We gave him a Ram.[4]

Besides Eminem what was special about this commercial?

I think what is very important in this commercial was the choir. The choir is a gospel choir called, "Selected of God" and they are pure Detroit. I didn't bring them, to be honest, just a casting agency, cast them, you know, cast them and found them in some church and brought them. And now I am going to tell you a little antidote that I have never told anyone and I don't know why, I just happen to not tell anyone. It's nice, very cute. In brainstorming we said okay, we have the music, we have this beautiful script with Eminem opening the door and saying "This is the Motor City and this is what we do." We missed something, we wanted something more, we wanted something more magical, we want something more authentic and that's where this crazy idea of having a Detroit Gospel Choir singing "Lose Yourself." That [idea] came 48 hours before shooting. Someone cast this choir and worked on the arrangements of this gospel. We worked hard making the gospel choir version "Lose Yourself," which is a little piece you can hear in the commercial because that is where we thought back to magic and wisdom and so that's where you could have so much more emotion and authenticity. And speaking of authenticity and that's the little antidote that I want to tell you. So once we have worked out this gospel arrangement and we teach the choir how to sing it and we bring them on the stage of the Fox Theatre which is a landmark we decided not tell them that Eminem would be in the commercial and that Eminem would physically walk into the Fox Theatre and get on the stage with them. These are the most humble people ever. We are really speaking about a choir of a church in downtown Detroit. These are people who never traveled in their life. They never tried to make a career or to end up in a commercial. Now they are famous. At the time, they weren't looking at anything of this kind. And clearly for people like this meeting with Eminem was something inconceivable, just simply inconceivable. And being in a commercial together with Eminem is totally inconceivable. So what you see in the commercial is something which we captured totally live and we told them to start singing. So they sing their piece, "Lose Yourself," the gospel version and in a totally unprompted way, unscripted, without notice, without letting them know you have Eminem getting on the stage and we wanted to capture their reaction. It is like candid camera. We wanted to see what would happen, would they stop singing, would they start screaming, "Oh my God." We wanted to see what would happen and what I think is incredible is that nothing happened. They were so professional. I don't know what happened in their heads. They saw Eminem in flesh and bones walking towards them and getting on stage and singing with them, I don't know what is with their minds while they were singing. What you see is really, was not scripted, is just one take and they just keep singing. They are big now. I wanted to make them a star and they are now and it is great. I brought them with me to New York on another auto show and they started singing in front of a crowd of journalists and that was unbelievable. Everyone was so moved. It was almost a joke having them sing the song that we worked out two days before and sing it and the real Eminem

comes, flesh and bones, and delivered his line while they are singing. And that was incredible.[5]

1. Keys: "Emotion and Authenticity." Olivier Francois
2. "I don't believe in using celebrities and famous people just for the
   sake of it ... Their story has to make sense in the story of the ad."
   Olivier Francois
3. Helps to have a hometown artist who cares.

Chrysler Commercial Copy

I got a question for you.

What does this city know about luxury?

What does a town that's been to hell and back know about the finer
things in life?

I'll tell you, more than most!

You see, it's the hottest fires that make the hardest steel, add hard work
and conviction.

And the know how that runs generations deep in every last one of us.

That's who we are.

That's our story.

Now it's probably not the one you've been reading in the papers.

The one being written by folks who have never even been here and
don't know what we're capable of.

Because when it comes to luxury, it's as much about where it's from as
who it's for.

Now we're from America. But this isn't New York City. Or the Windy
City. Or Sin City. And we're certainly no one's Emerald City.

This is the Motor City. And this is what we do.

CHAPTER 20

Horses and Dogs…
Fleetwood Mac, Passenger, and Budweiser (2013 and 2014)

Used with permission of Anheuser-Busch LLC.

It is appropriate to finish with Budweiser since this is the only brand with two commercials. Of the first in 2013 it was written: "It's a poignant and well-shot commercial—in keeping with some of the better Budweiser ads through the years—made all the more evocative by the use of Fleetwood Mac's 'Landslide.'"[1] And of the second in 2014 it was said: "This spot is anchored by a strong musical choice. Last year it was Fleetwood Mac's 'Landslide.' This time it is 'Let Her Go' by Passenger."[2] The second one may have been even more excellent than the first.

The matchup on the football field was seemingly decided about 12 seconds after kickoff, and the battle to decide the best Super Bowl commercial has also been a landslide. Budweiser, their famous Clydesdale horses and a very adorable puppy have claimed the top prize according to a variety of metrics. Anheuser-Busch's "Puppy Love" ad, developed by the agency Anomaly, was voted the top commercial during the game by viewers on Hulu. It also earned the top spot on USA Today's Ad Meter, which is calculated through online surveys of Super Bowl viewers each year. The spot is also dominating the other ads on YouTube, where it has racked up more than 37 million views since Wednesday, and it's easily lapping the other ads in terms of social activity, according to media metrics firm iSpot.[3]

The person directly responsible for both ads is Paul Chibe. Chibe is the former vice president U.S. Marketing and U.S. chief marketing officer at Anheuser-Busch. Billboard named him No. 14 on its 2014 Billboard Power 100. He was responsible for all things music including the Budweiser "Made in America" tour.

Brand sponsorship of U.S. live music and events reached a record high of $1.3 billion in 2013, according to analytics firm IEG, further cementing the importance of marketing dollars as a crucial revenue stream for artists, promoters and labels. Not only was Anheuser-Busch the highest-ranked brand in terms of dollars spent—bypassing Pepsi and Coca-Cola for the first time with upwards of $200 million spent on events and venue sponsorship.[4]

Chibe commented on both award-winning ads beginning with 2013:

Let me go back to the first one where we used Stevie Nicks. Whenever you are developing advertising, at least the way we do it in Anheuser-Busch which is consistent with us and other companies, is you go through a process of you write a brief, then in that brief you call out what your needs are for from an advertising standpoint, what your main message is, what you want it to be and all that. Then when the agency comes back with the concepts, what they want to present as the ad ideas. When it came to the Stevie Nick's song that was something that the ad agency Anomaly had identified very early on. We used it in the anoma. There were things that really scared us because we liked the song so much was whether or not we would get approval because Stevie Nicks, as far as I remember, had never approved prior to that use in commercial use for any of her songs or that song had never been used in advertising, Landslide. So one of the things we did was we wanted to make sure that when you saw the ad, you would see that we were presenting something that was very respectful and very true to the song. We obviously had to find some backups just in case but when the agency approached her and showed her the ad idea, basically a rough cut on the ad with the song in it, she loved it and approved it. I think a part of it was it was a positive experience and I think that is something that when you are working with artist, there are some artists that would never sign with their music, and there are artists that will sign their music. I think that an advertiser, like A-B (Anheuser-Busch) or anyone else, what you want to do is show consistently that you respect the music and you are going to treat it well in your work because not everyone would want to have a personal approval, would sign something off. I think that builds your reputation of being a marker who uses music in advertising well, and that permits you to get approvals for the future.[5]

Chibe continued that the 2014 commercial didn't have a definitive song at the beginning:

We did have some different tracks in mind ("We looked at 'Ho Hey' which is by the Lumineers"), and then what happened is then we found that track ("Let Her Go") and we liked it and it did phenomenally well. Even in the last week though there was some back and forth on whether or not that would be the track on the commercial for the Super Bowl. Myself, and the guy that works for me, the VP of Budweiser in the US, we held the line like this is the song, this is the song that we like and we are going to keep it. Then we cut that song and I felt that it was a very powerful, a very evocative song that captured the commercial extremely well. Because the thing that I think a lot of people realized, music is just as evocative as the imaginary and if you don't have the right music, you can take the spot that would perform extremely well and make it an average ad or a less than average ad.[6]

When asked what makes an excellent popular music in advertising campaign, Chibe said:

An excellent campaign must always drive forward your business objectives against the brand. So there are plenty of cool commercials that I like that when you talk to the people that were involved, haven't necessarily done anything for the brand. So one of the things you want to see are improvement in the consideration ladder liking in brand loyalty, top brand loyalty, or top favorite brand loyalty, you want to see improvement in those dimensions along with improvement in brand performance. So the thing is that when you think about music, I think, the way to think about your advertising is to grow in the things that are relevant and important to people as being a part of people's lives. People express themselves with music. People self-identify very often, with the group you are hanging around with. If you could think about young people, the younger punk rocker type, or if you are into EDM or Grunge, or if you go back to the time when I was in college, people created a lot of their self-identity with the music affinity and you have to remember music is an emotionally extremely powerful device. If you take that emotion and combine it with visual imagery that has relevance to your brand, you could drive your brand. You really create a meaning and you borrow that meaning from the music and install it against your brand. I think when you see what Anheuser-Busch has done with it, we've used it extremely successfully. I have been interviewed on this stuff too and some people see the connection like this is a tool, you have to use the tools at hand to create the right connection and I think people are starting to see how positive it is.[7]

1. "You want to show consistently that you respect the music and you are going to treat it well in your work." Paul Chibe

2. "Music is just as evocative as the imaginary and if you don't have the right music, you can take the spot that would perform extremely well and make it an average ad or a less than average ad. You can take an average ad with extremely powerful music and make it an amazing commercial." Paul Chibe

3. "If you take emotion and combine it with visual imagery that has relevance to your brand, you could drive your brand. You really create a meaning and you borrow that meaning from the music and install it against your brand." Paul Chibe

Encore: The Bands

Moby regretted it.

Sting was ok with the first time but didn't want to do it again.

Dylan just needed to be asked.

Eminem needed to be convinced.

Paul McCartney is probably still mad at Michael Jackson.

The bands that lent their songs to the brands in this book did so for different reasons and with mixed feelings. All of them benefited financially through licensing fees. For some, like Dirty Vegas, it took music and the group to a place it may not have been able to go without it. For others, like Sting it took music that was dead and gave it life through exposure. And for still others, like Drake, it gave his music life and audience after his death. Some that were hesitant at first, like the Rolling Stones or Led Zeppelin, embraced it after it was released. Some like Moby who fully embraced it in the beginning, regretted it later. Some thoroughly enjoyed it like Bob Dylan (what's not to like?).

All the bands have one thing in common. They all decided, for whatever reason, to do it. To let their music be heard again, or in some cases for the first time, with a brand that valued it so much that it was willing to marry its brand with that band. The bands took a greater risk certainly. What would their fans think? The answer is that some fans liked it and some didn't. But they kept buying their music and attending their concerts. The brands took a risk too. What if no one noticed? What if everyone noticed but not for the right reasons? The answer is the same. Some liked it and some didn't but the brand kept playing on.

When it works it works, popular music in advertising that is. For the 20 bands and brands in this book it worked. They got paid and they got exposed. When there was a creative vision by a brand for a band (like

Victoria's Secret), or band for a brand (like Sting) it felt good. Not forced but natural, almost meant to be together. Maybe a prearranged marriage, but they fell in love, or at least in like. They became the 20 most popular songs and brands of all time.

Notes

Opening Act: The Brands

1. ABInBev (2013).
2. MarketingCharts (2014).
3. Kia Media (2013).
4. Wong (2010).
5. Wong (2010).
6. Wong (2010).
7. Wong (2010).
8. Kiley (2011a).
9. Howard (2004).
10. GrabStats (2012).
11. Diaz and Pathak (2013).
12. Zatorre and Salimpoor (2013).

Chapter 1

1. Ryan (2012).
2. Backer (1993), p. 83.
3. Backer (1993).
4. Interview with Bill Backer June 05, 2013.
5. Moye (2013).
6. Backer (1993), p. 24.
7. Interview with Bill Backer June 05, 2013.
8. Interview with Joe Belliotti July 23, 2013.
9. Interview with Joe Belliotti July 23, 2013.
10. Interview with Joe Belliotti July 23, 2013.
11. Interview with Bill Backer June 5, 2013.
12. Backer (1993), p. 276.
13. Interview with Bill Backer June 05, 2013.
14. Interview with Bill Backer June 05, 2013.
15. Interview with Bill Backer June 05, 2013.

Chapter 2

1. Herrera (2009).
2. Herrera (2009).

3. Interview with Roger Enrico January 10, 2014.
4. Interview with Roger Enrico January 10, 2014.
5. Interview with Roger Enrico January 10, 2014.
6. Interview with Roger Enrico January 10, 2014.
7. Interview with Roger Enrico January 10, 2014.
8. Interview with Roger Enrico January 10, 2014.
9. Interview with Roger Enrico January 10, 2014.
10. Interview with Roger Enrico January 10, 2014.
11. Interview with Roger Enrico January 10, 2014.
12. Interview with Roger Enrico January 10, 2014.
13. Miller (2012).

Chapter 3

1. Interview with Seth Werner February 27, 2014.
2. Interview with Seth Werner February 27, 2014.
3. Interview with Seth Werner February 27, 2014.
4. Interview with Seth Werner February 27, 2014.
5. Interview with Seth Werner February 27, 2014.
6. Interview with Seth Werner February 27, 2014.
7. Interview with Seth Werner February 27, 2014.
8. Interview with Seth Werner February 27, 2014.
9. "The 50 Best Commercials of All Time" (1997).

Chapter 4

1. Doyle (2008a).
2. Pareles (1987).
3. "The Basics of Business History" (1999).

Chapter 5

1. Doyle (2010a).
2. Doyle (2010b)
3. Denardo (2012).
4. Denardo (2012).
5. Interview with Len Peltier April 30, 2014.
6. Interview with Len Peltier April 30, 2014.
7. Interview with Len Peltier April 30, 2014.

Chapter 6

1. Holden (1986).
2. Gazdik (1998).
3. Halpert (2011).
4. Interview with Kurt Ritter June 13, 2013.
5. Lacy (2013).
6. Lacy (2013).

Chapter 7

1. Interview with Robert (Bob) Herbold March 5, 2014.
2. Scott (2011).
3. Scott (2011).
4. Scott (2011).
5. Interview with (Bob) Herbold March 5, 2014.

Chapter 8

1. Sting.com: Discography (2013).
2. Interview with Copeland June 6, 2013.
3. Interview with Sting June 21, 2013.
4. Sting.com: Discography (2013).
5. Interview with Sting June 21, 2013.
6. Donaton (2003).
7. Donaton (2004).
8. Donaton (2003).
9. Jaguar Heritage (2013).
10. Wernie (2000).
11. Wernie (2000).
12. Interview with Saltiel June 20, 2013.
13. Interview with Murphy June 14, 2013.
14. Wernie (2000).
15. Doyle (2008b).
16. Interview with Saltiel June 20, 2013.
17. Interview with Saltiel June 20, 2013.
18. Interview with Saltiel June 20, 2013.
19. Interview with Copeland June 6, 2013.
20. Interview with Sting June 21, 2013.
21. Wernie (2000).
22. Interview with Copeland June 6, 2013.

23. Allan (2005).
24. Powers (2000).
25. Interview with Copeland June 6, 2013.
26. Interview with Copeland June 6, 2013.
27. Donaton (2003).
28. Doyle (2008b).
29. Doyle (2008b).
30. Doyle (2008b).
31. Doyle (2008b).
32. Doyle (2008b).
33. Interview with Saltiel July 25, 2013.
34. Donaton (2003).
35. Donaton (2003).
36. Customer Reviews for Sting. (2010).
37. Sting.com: Tour, Symphonicity. (2013).
38. Haar (2011).
39. "Jaguar TV Ad's Greatest Hits" (2007).

Chapter 9

1. Vaziri (2000).
2. Vaziri (2000).
3. Alan Pafenbach: Creative Direction (2009).
4. Interview with Alan Pafenback January 7, 2014.
5. Interview with Alan Pafenback January 7, 2014.
6. Interview with Alan Pafenback January 7, 2014.
7. Interview with Alan Pafenback January 7, 2014.
8. Interview with Alan Pafenback January 7, 2014.
9. Interview with Joe Boyd July 30, 2013.
10. Interview with Joe Boyd July 30, 2013.
11. Interview with Joe Boyd July 30, 2013.
12. Interview with Joe Boyd July 30, 2013.
13. Lloyd (2009).

Chapter 10

1. Weingarten (2009).
2. Tyrangiel (2001).
3. Weingarten (2009).
4. Smith (2002).
5. m2.com (2000)
6. Leiby (2000).

7. Leiby (2000).
8. Leiby (2000).
9. Weingarten (2009).
10. Weingarten (2009).

Chapter 11

1. Interview with Eric Hirshberg August 12, 2013.
2. Cumberpatch (2002).
3. Interview with Steve Smith August 1, 2013.
4. Interview with Steve Smith August 1, 2013.
5. Interview with Mike Sheldon August 1, 2013.
6. Interview with Eric Hirshberg August 12, 2013.
7. Interview with Pierre Gagnon August 8, 2013.
8. Troha (2012).
9. Interview with Mike Shelton August 1, 2013.
10. Interview with Eric Hirshberg August 12, 2013.
11. Interview with Pierre Gagnon August 8, 2013.
12. Interview with Steve Smith August 1, 2013.
13. Halliday (2002).
14 Interview with Pierre Gagnon August 8, 2013.
15. Interview with Eric Hirshberg August 12, 2013.
16. Interview with Eric Hirshberg August 12, 2013.
17. Interview with Pierre Gagnon August 8, 2013.
18. Interview with Eric Hirshberg August 12, 2013.
19. Interview with Eric Hirshberg August 12, 2013.
20. Interview with Mike Shelton August 1, 2013.
21. Interview with Eric Hirshberg August 12, 2013.
22. Interview with Steve Smith August 1, 2013.
23. Interview with Pierre Gagnon August 8, 2013.

Chapter 12

1. Hopperd (2011).
2. Stevenson (2005).
3. Interview with Lisa Bauer July 9, 2013.
4. Interview with Lisa Bauer July 9, 2013.
5. Interview with Lisa Bauer July 9, 2013.
6. Interview with Lisa Bauer July 9, 2013.
7. Interview with Lisa Bauer July 9, 2013.
8. Klein (2009).

Chapter 13

1. Jackson (2010).
2. *Wikipedia* (2014).
3. Interview with Jay Spenchian June 13, 2013.
4. Interview with Jay Spenchian June 13, 2013.

Chapter 14

1. Isaacson (2001).
2. Doyle (2011).

Chapter 15

1. Howard (2004).
2. Howard (2004).
3. Howard (2004).
4. Interview with Ed Razek March 5, 2014.

Chapter 16

1. Interview with Chuck Gamble January 14, 2014.
2. Interview with Chuck Gamble January 14, 2014.
3. Interview with Chuck Gamble January 14, 2014.
4. Interview with Chuck Gamble January 14, 2014.
5. Interview with Chuck Gamble January 14, 2014.

Chapter 17

1. Archambault (2006).
2. Abcarian (2006).
3. Archambault (2006).
4. Abcarian (2006).
5. Interview with Steve Scharf March 5, 2014.

Chapter 18

1. Crupi (2009).
2. Interview with Michael Sprague December 10, 2013.
3. Interview with Michael Sprague December 10, 2013.

4. Interview with Michael Sprague December 10, 2014.
5. Interview with Colin Jeffery January 15, 2014.
6. Interview with Colin Jeffery January 15, 2014.

Chapter 19

1. Kiley (2011b).
2. Kiley (2011b).
3. Kiley (2011b).
4. Interview with Olivier Francois June 21, 2013.
5. Interview with Olivier Francois June 21, 2013.

Chapter 20

1. Nudd (2014).
2. Nudd (2014).
3. Luckerson (2014).
4. Hampp (2014).
5. Interview with Paul Chibe April 9, 2014.
6. Interview with Paul Chibe April 9, 2014.
7. Interview with Paul Chibe April 9, 2014.

References

"Jaguar TV Ad's Greatest Hits." February 20, 2007. Rhapsody Radish.

"The 50 Best Commercials of All Time." 1997. *Entertainment Weekly*, March 28. http://www.ew.com/ew/article/0,,287305,00.html

"The Basics of Business History." May 19, 1999. The Street. http://www.thestreet.com/story/747904/1.html

Abcarian, R. 2006. "Love It or Hate It: A 'Fair Lady' in Gap's Skinny Pants." *Los Angeles Times*, September 23. http://articles.latimes.com/2006/sep/23/entertainment/et-gap23

ABInBev. 2013. http://www.ab-inbev.com/pdf/AR13/AB_InBev_AR_consumer_insights.pdf

Alan Pafenbach: Creative Direction. 2009. http://alanpafenbach.com/

Allan, D. 2005. "An Essay on Popular Music in Advertising: Bankruptcy of Culture or Marriage of Art and Commerce." *Advertising and Society* 6, no. 1.

Archambault, E. 2006. "New Gap Marketing Campaign Featuring Original Film Footage of Audrey Hepburn Helps Gap 'Keeps it Simple' This Fall." http://www.prnewswire.com/news-releases/new-gap-marketing-campaign-featuring-original-film-footage-of-audrey-hepburn-helps-gap-keeps-it-simple-this-fall-55899262.html

Backer, B. 1993. *The Care and Feeding of Ideas*. New York: Times, Books-Random House.

Crupi, A. 2009. "Kia's Soul Finds 'New Way to Roll.'" *Adweek*, February 26. http://www.adweek.com/news/advertising-branding/kias-soul-finds-new-way-roll-98514

Cumberpatch, F. July 2, 2002. "Dirty Vegas: Last Night a DJ Sold My Car." MTV.com http://www.mtv.com/news/1454923/days-go-by-and-still-you-cant-get-dirty-vegas-out-of-your-head/

Customer Reviews for Sting. 2010. Ticketmaster. http://reviews.ticketmaster.com/7171/723578/sting-reviews/reviews.htm? page=51&sort= submissionTime

Denardo, M. 2012. "Levi's Hit Machine." *Daily Front Row*, February 9. http://explore.levi.com/news/style/levis_hit_machine_len_peltier/

Diaz, A.C., and S. Pathak. 2013. "10 Brands That Made Music Part of Their Marketing DNA." *Advertising Age*, September 30. http://adage.com/article/special-report-music-and-marketing/licensing-10-brands-innovating-music/244336/

Donaton, S. 2003. "The Story Behind a Landmark Music Commercial: How Miles Copeland Brought Sting and Jaguar Together." *Advertising Age*,

September. http://adage.com/article/viewpoint/advertising-landmark-jaguar
-sting-tv-commercial/38400/

Donaton, S. 2004. *Madison & Vine: Why the Entertainment and Advertising Industries Must Converge to Survive.* McGraw-Hill.

Doyle, J. September 27, 2008a. "Nike & The Beatles, 1987–1989." PopHistoryDig.com, http://www.pophistorydig.com/?p=702

Doyle, J. September 27, 2008b. "Sting & Jaguar, 1999–2001." PopHistoryDig. com, http://www.pophistorydig.com/?p=612

Doyle, J. November 1, 2010a. "Levi's Be My Baby, 1989 TV Ad." PopHistoryDig. com http://www.pophistorydig.com/?p=7532

Doyle, J. January 18, 2010b. "Be My Baby, 1960s–2010." PopHistoryDig.com http://www.pophistorydig.com/?p=5201

Doyle, J. December 9, 2011. "The iPod Silhouettes: 2000–2011." PopHistoryDig. com http://www.pophistorydig.com/?tag=apple-silhouette-ads

Gazdik, T. 1998. "Donald Gould, Creator of Chevy's 'Like a Rock' Concept, Dies at 54." *Adweek*, June 1. http://www.adweek.com/news/advertising/ donald-gould-creator-chevys-rock-concept-dies-54-45319

GrabStats. 2012. http://www.grabstats.com/statmain.aspx?StatID=110

Haar, P.V. 2011. "Last Night: Sting at Verizon Wireless Theatre." *Houston Press*, November 18. http://blogs.houstonpress.com/rocks/2011/11/sting_verizon _wireless_theater.php

Halliday, J. 2002. "British Band Makes U.S. Debut in Car Commercial." *Advertising Age*, March 11. http://adage.com/article/news/advertising-dirty -vegas-makes-debut-mitsubishi-campaign/33972/

Halpert, J. 2011. "Chevy's Most Enduring Advertising Campaigns: How the Ideas Took Root." *Advertising Age*, October 31. http://adage.com/article/ special-report-chevy-100/chevy-s-campaign-ideas-root/230682/

Hampp, A. 2014. "Paul Chibe: The 2014 Billboard Power 100." *Billboardbiz*, January 15. http://www.billboard.com/biz/5869783/paul-chibe-the-2014 -billboard-power-100

Herrera, M. 2009. "Michael Jackson, Pepsi Made Marketing History." *Adweek*, July 6. http://www.adweek.com/news/advertising-branding/michael-jackson -pepsi-made-marketing-history-99789

Holden, S. 1986. "The Pop Life; Bob Seger's View of Life and Loving." *The New York Times*, May 14. http://www.nytimes.com/1986/05/14/arts/the-pop-life -bob-seger-s-view-of-life-and-loving.html

Hopperd, D. April 13, 2011. "The 20 Most Inappropriate Songs Ever Used in Commercials." vH1.com http://www.vh1.com/celebrity/2011-04-13/the -20-most-inappropriate-songs-ever-used-in-commercials/

Howard, T. 2004. "Dylan Ad for Underwear Generates Lingering Buzz." *USA Today*, May 16. http://usatoday30.usatoday.com/money/advertising/adtrack /2004-05-16-victoria-secrets-dylan_x.htm

Isaacson, W. 2001. *Steve Jobs.* New York: Simon and Shuster.

Jackson, J. 2010. "Jimmy Page on Led Zeppelin IV, the Band's Peak and Their Reunion." *The Sunday Times*, January 8. http://entertainment.timesonline.co.uk/tol/arts_and_entertainment/music/article6979690.ece

Jaguar Heritage. 2013. http://www.jaguarheritage.org/JaguarHistory_Menu.aspx

Kia Media. 2013. http://www.kiamedia.com/us/en/media/pressreleases/5520/michael-sprague

Kiley, D. February 21, 2011a. "How Chrysler Chief Olivier Francois Is Selling Detroit." *Advertising Age* http://adage.com/article/news/chrysler-chief-olivier-francois-selling-detroit/148999/

Kiley, D. February 8, 2011b. "The Inside Story: Chrysler's Risky Eminem Super Bowl Commercial." Aol Autos http://autos.aol.com/article/chrysler-eminem-super-bowl-ad/

Klein, B. 2009. *As Heard on TV: Popular Music in Advertising*. Ashgate.

Lacy, E. 2013. "Bob Seger Resurrects 'Like a Rock' Chevrolet Commercial Song After 27-year Absence from Tour; Detroit Fans in for Treat." MLive. http://www.mlive.com/news/detroit/index.ssf/2013/04/bob_seger_resurrects_like_a_ro.html

Leiby, R. 2000. "Blues News: International News." *The Washington Post*, August 9. http://www.blues.co.nz/news/article.php?id=341

Lloyd. 2009. "Commercial of the Decade: Nick Drake, 'Pink Moon,' and a Smart Little Volkswagen." The Brown Tweed. http://thebrowntweedsociety.com/2009/12/28/nick-drake-volkswagen-commercial/

Luckerson, V. 2014. "This Was the Most Successful Commercial of the Super Bowl." *Time*, February 3. http://time.com/3870/budweiser-puppy-love-super-bowl-commercial/

m2.com. 2000. http://www.m2.com/m2/web/story.php/2000060FA8FEA2F774A9802568F800319F57

MarketingCharts. 2014. http://www.marketingcharts.com/wp/traditional/super-bowl-2014-ads-facts-and-figures-39421/

Miller, M. September 18, 2012. "Where There's Pepsi, There's Michael Jackson." Brandchannel http://www.brandchannel.com/home/post/2012/09/18/Pepsi-Michael-Jackson-Bad-25th-091812.aspx

Moye, J. July 15, 2013. "5 Facts About Coke's 5-Note Melody" http://www.coca-colacompany.com/coca-cola-music/5-facts-about-cokes-5-note-melody

Nudd, T. 2014. "Budweiser's Super Bowl Spot Reunites a Clydesdale with Its Breeder." *Adweek*, January 31. http://www.adweek.com/news/advertising-branding/budweisers-super-bowl-spot-reunites-clydesdale-its-breeder-146910

Pareles, J. 1987. "Nike Calls Beatles Suit Groundless." *The New York Times*, April 5. http://www.nytimes.com/1987/08/05/arts/nike-calls-beatles-suit-groundless.html

Powers, A. 2000. "Pop Review; It's Sting's World: Exoticism, Torchy Balads and the Good Life." *The New York Times*, September 14. http://www.nytimes.

com/2000/09/14/arts/pop-review-it-s-sting-s-world-exoticism-torchy
-ballads-and-the-good-life.html

Ryan, T. January 1, 2012. "The Making of "I'd Like to Buy the World a Coke."
http://www.coca-colacompany.com/stories/coke-lore-hilltop-story

Scott, A. July 6, 2011. "How Bill Gates and Mick Jagger Struck a Deal on Windows
95 Launch." *Puget Sound Business Journal* http://www.bizjournals.com/
seattle/blog/techflash/2011/06/bill-gates-mick-jagger-deal.html?page=all

Smith, E. 2002. "Organization Moby." Wired. http://www.wired.com/wired/
archive/10.05/moby_pr.html

Stevenson, S. 2005. "What's the Worst Ad Song Ever?" *Slate*, June 6. http://www.
slate.com/articles/business/ad_report_card/2005/06/whats_the_worst_ad_
song_ever.html

Sting.com: Discography. 2013. http://sting.com/discography/index/ablum/
albumId/9/tagName/Albums

Sting.com: Tour, Symphonicity. 2013. http://sting.com/tour/date/id/2528

Troha, M. 2012. "Throwback Thursday: 2003 Mitsubishi Eclipse 'Days Go
By' Commercial feat. Dirty Vegas." http://tier10lab.com/2012/10/25/
throwback-thursday-2003-mitsubishi-eclipse-days-go-by-commercial
-featuring-dirty-vegas/

Tyrangiel, J. 2001. "Music for the Masses." *Time*, July 30. http://content.time
.com/time/world/article/0,8599,2047741,00.html

Vaziri, A. 2000. "Nick Drake's 'Pink Moon' is Rising." *Rolling Stone*, April 11.
http://www.rollingstone.com/music/news/nick-drakes-pink-moon-is
-rising-20000411

Weingarten, C. 2009. "'Play' 10 Years Later: Moby's Track by Track Guide to
1999's Global Smash." *Rolling Stone*, July 2. http://www.rollingstone.com/
music/news/play-10-years-later-mobys-track-by-track-guide-to-1999s
-global-smash-20090702

Wernie, B. March 27, 2000. "Jaguar S-type Evokes Feeling of Style and Success,
Says Rock Star Sting." *Automotive News Europe* 5, no. 7, p. 18.

Wikipedia. 2014. http://en.wikipedia.org/wiki/Rock_and_Roll_%28Led_
Zeppelin_song%29

Wong, E. 2010. "Names You Need to Know: Kia Motors America's Michael
Sprague." *Forbes*. http://www.forbes.com/sites/elainewong/2010/12/22/
names-you-need-to-know-kia-motor-co-s-michael-sprague/

Zatorre, R.J., and V.N. Salimpoor. 2013. "Why Music Makes Our Brain Sing."
The New York Times, June 7. http://www.nytimes.com/2013/06/09/opinion/
sunday/why-music-makes-our-brain-sing.html?_r=0

Bibliography

Burns, G. 1996. "Popular Music, Television, and Generational Identity." *Journal of Popular Culture* 30, no. 3, pp. 129–41.

Levitin, D. 2007. *This is Your Brain on Music*. New York: Penguin.

McChesney, R. 2001. "Money for Nothing." The Media Education Foundation. Videocassette.

Wayshak, M. 2014. "What You Could Learn from Budweiser's Heart-Melting Ad." *Entrepreneur*. http://www.entrepreneur.com/article/231203

Index